W9-CAD-234

WORKING
WITH
DIFFICULT PEOPLE

William Lundin, Ph.D.
Kathleen Lundin

amacom

AMERICAN MANAGEMENT ASSOCIATION

THE WORKSMART SERIES

New York • Atlanta • Boston • Chicago • Kansas City • San Francisco • Washington, D.C.
Brussels • Toronto • Mexico City

This book is available at a special
discount when ordered in bulk quantities.
For information, contact Special Sales Department,
AMACOM, a division of American Management Association,
135 West 50th Street, New York, NY 10020.

This publication is designed to provide accurate and authoritative information in regard to the subject matter covered. It is sold with the understanding that the publisher is not engaged in rendering legal,
accounting, or other professional service. If legal advice or other expert
assistance is required, the services of a competent professional person
should be sought.

Library of Congress Cataloging-in-Publication Data

Lundin, William, 1923–
    Working with difficult people / William Lundin, Kathleen Lundin.
        p.   cm.—(WorkSmart series)
    Includes bibliographical references (p.).
    ISBN 0-8144-7838-7
    1. Conflict management—Case studies.   2. Interpersonal relations—
Case studies.   3. Interpersonal conflict—Case studies.
I. Lundin, Kathleen, 1935– .   II. Title.   III. Series.
HD42.L86   1995
650.1'3—dc20   95-24862
                                                              CIP

© 1995 AMACOM, a division of
American Management Association, New York.
All rights reserved.
Printed in the United States of America.

This publication may not be reproduced,
stored in a retrieval system,
or transmitted in whole or in part,
in any form or by any means, electronic,
mechanical, photocopying, recording, or otherwise,
without the prior written permission of AMACOM,
a division of American Management Association,
135 West 50th Street, New York, NY 10020.

Printing number

10   9   8   7   6   5   4   3   2   1

WORKING
WITH
DIFFICULT
PEOPLE

The WorkSmart Series

CONTENTS

WORKING
WITH
DIFFICULT
PEOPLE

INTRODUCTION

Which of these statements do you agree with?

Difficult people . . .
Make my life miserable. ____
Reduce my morale. ____
Get me angry. ____
Deplete my energies. ____
Make me feel helpless. ____
Ruin a good thing. ____
Make me scream. ____
Affect my productivity. ____
Waste my time. ____
Are insidious. ____

And that may be only the beginning. Dealing with someone else's irritating behavior can really waste your time and sap your energy. For many of us, dealing with the stress and frustrations of other people has become so commonplace that it is considered normal—the way things are.

Well, things don't have to be difficult. You can do something positive about difficult people in your workplace. This book will show you how to remake *your* attitude and behavior. The difficult person will still be there, but you will be less of a target. You, not the other person, will be in charge of the interaction.

The spread of restructuring and downsizing has increased the amount of stress most employees have to cope with today because their future is less certain than it was in the past. And at the same time, employers are asking workers to produce more than ever before, with fewer people to share the workload. It's no wonder that people are becoming difficult to deal with.

What have you noticed in your own workplace? Are your coworkers becoming touchier? More easily angered? More suspicious? Are they on edge? This state of affairs is all too common, perhaps the unavoidable result of the rapid rate of change in today's workplace and society in general.

In this unsettled environment, knowing how to handle difficult people and their disruptive behavior is one of the most important skills you can have. It will help you become a more valuable employee and a more self-reliant person. By mastering the techniques set out in this book, you will increase both your energy and optimism. You'll see how to overcome the hurdles thrown down by difficult people and how to develop skills that can enrich both your work and private life.

HOW THIS BOOK WILL HELP YOU DEAL WITH DIFFICULT PEOPLE

Some people are *and always will be* difficult; their irritating behavior is fixed deep within their personalities. Others—in fact, most people—are upsetting to us only from time to time. But unless you know the person very well, it is not easy to recognize the difference—whether the annoying behavior is deep-seated or mostly situational—nor should you try. Your concern is how to handle disruptive behavior by getting a fresh fix on your own attitudes and reactions, not figuring out underlying causes of the other person's difficult behavior.

While you cannot (and should not) expect to become a counselor to your coworkers, you can become more sensitive to them and learn how to befriend a coworker in need. Specifically, this book explains a system that will teach you to:

- Understand your reaction to a difficult person.
- Explore your attitudes and why you react as you do.
- Practice healthier responses to those who are making your life miserable.

To do our best work, we all need a level playing field, free of snares, thickets, traps, and drive-by emotional shootings. This book will help you create that level playing field by exploring specific ways to approach and respond to difficult people.

AN EASY-TO-LEARN FORMAT

There are countless difficult behaviors (and during the past thirty years we've probably *worked with* most of them), and you can learn to deal with all of them. We have selected nine examples of difficult people taken from our case histories as teaching models. These case studies will help you see the difficult person as a reactive human being. He or she will be presented through the eyes of a coworker who has come to us for help and advice.

You will learn how to handle the difficult person by "listening in" to the questions, answers, comments, and advice between one of us (Kathy or Bill) and the co-worker seeking help. We will also use exercises to help the advice-seekers to understand themselves better, and occasionally interrupt the dialogue to add our own commentary and interpretation.

You are about to join us on a one-day adventure as we sort out difficult-people problems presented to us as a result of the ad we ran, which is reproduced below. You will learn, and remember, by watching and doing.

Here's the ad we ran:

DIFFICULT PEOPLE RUINING YOUR LIFE?

Bring us your problems. We'll show you how to handle them. Are you facing someone's anger and resentment? Is your co-worker too suspicious? Does your supervisor treat your ideas with cynicism? Is your team leader apathetic?

Aren't people listening? Is that aggressive, competitive guy getting all the rewards and attention? Do you come home washed-out and frustrated?

Our doors open at 8:00 A.M. No appointment is necessary, just show up with your story. The service is free under one condition: that you promise to do the exercises we recommend.

The next day we looked out our office window, and you would have thought we had advertised a free vacation for two. "Maybe," we said, looking for a reason for the massive turnout, "that's what navigating life is all about—learning how to work with difficult people."

Here is what happened as we met and listened to one aggravated co-worker after the next. . . .

CHAPTER 1

MEAN AND ANGRY

Anybody can become angry—that is easy; but to be angry with the right person, and to the right degree, and at the right time, and for the right purpose, and in the right way—that is not within everybody's power and is not easy.

—Aristotle

Anger has become fashionable. If you're not angry with someone, others will call you an unrealistic wimp. More anger than ever is being expressed at work and at home. Anger is not an invitation to dance. It's the opposite; it says, "Keep away; I'm dangerous. I might hurt you." Anger is meant to be intimidating, forcing the other person to give way, yield space, conform, become contrite and controllable. Anger subordinates all other feelings to lesser roles, and it freezes situations. It can come on like an explosion or a slowly rising tide. In any form, anger is meant to frighten and intimidate, and the secret of dealing with it is not to be afraid.

THE CASE OF MARGARET AND THE SNARLING SUPERVISOR

The first person in line is Margaret, a conservatively dressed woman of about forty-five, who works as a data entry supervisor in a bank. She is married with two grown children and is basically a happy person. Work has always given her satisfaction and a sense of accomplishment—until the past few months. She was promoted a few months ago, and now she's stuck with a new boss whom she describes as "a mean, nasty person who scowls at me as if I'm about to do something wrong."

Kathy: What's it doing to your work?

Margaret: It's more than my work. I'm afraid I'm going to lose my promotion. I can't afford to let that happen. I dread going to work, facing that—ugh!

Kathy: You used to be happy. Now you're not.

Margaret: My husband noticed it. I never believed that you could get infected by another person's anger like that. It's unreal.

Kathy: But you're not giving up on your new position, and you want to do something about it. Right?

Margaret: I don't know where to start. I can't confront him. Others have tried, and now they're gone—transferred, fired, or quit.

Kathy: Tell me about a typical experience with your new boss.

Margaret: Well, I'm all right when I start to work—things to do and check, calls to return. You know. At about 10 A.M., just as I'm all straightened out and my people are working smoothly, *he* appears. "What are you doing? I gotta see you, now," he growls. It's that look. Not so much the words but the way he talks, like a threat and a prediction, like, "I know you're going to screw up." And he's getting himself angry in advance.

Kathy: It's clear that you're trapped. Can you describe what that kind of experience does to you? How does it make you feel?

Margaret: I'm on edge the rest of the day. I lose my temper with my staff, and that never happened before. I try to control it and tell myself it's him, not me. But I dwell on it, not knowing when he'll appear again. My people don't deserve to be upset because I'm upset, but I can't always control myself.

Kathy: Do you turn out as much work as you used to? Less work? What about the quality?

Margaret: That's what's so disgusting about the whole thing. We do less work. Who wouldn't? So he gets even angrier. As for the quality, what do you think?

Kathy: Well you're right, the problem is not you, it's what he's doing to you. Let's see if we can figure out a way for you to keep your job, get back to your previous efficiency, and lead your own life once again. The first thing I'd like you to do is fill out this questionnaire.

ANGER QUESTIONNAIRE

Complete the following questionnaire as it relates to your own experiences and feelings.

1. Why do people get angry? _____

2. What situations make you most angry? Please list three.

   _____

   _____

   _____

3. Describe how you feel when your anger is over.

   _____

4. How do people express anger where you work?

   _____

5. Have you ever been on the receiving end of a superior's anger?   Yes _____ No _____

6. Describe how it made you feel? _____

   _____

7. Did it affect your work?   Yes _____ No _____

   7a. How long? _____

8. In your position as a supervisor or manager, have you ever become openly angry with an employee?   Yes _____ No _____

   8a. Generally, for how long? _____

9. At times is open anger the only way to handle a situation at work?   Yes _____ No _____

10. Think of the most miserable boss you've ever known. Describe him or her.

_____

11. Do you think someone like that could become a nicer person?　　Yes _____ No _____

12. If "yes," what would it take? _____

13. Is anger part of the way things are in your company?　　Yes _____ No _____

　　13a. If "yes," what would it take to get that

Kathy gives the Anger Questionnaire in the box to Margaret. (The questionnaires in the boxes throughout this book are for you to fill out.) Here are Margaret's responses:

1. Why do people get angry? _Because they are angry with themselves._
2. What situations make you most angry? Please list three.
   People lying to me.
   Being disrespectful.
   People not pulling their load.
3. Describe how you feel when your anger is over. _Ashamed that I didn't handle the situation better._
4. How do people express anger where you work? _With angry looks._
5. Have you ever been on the receiving end of a superior's anger? Yes _X_ No ___
6. Describe how it made you feel? _Like retaliating._
7. Did it affect your work? Yes _X_ No ___
   7a. How long? _Sometimes almost a week._
8. In your position as a supervisor or manager, have you ever become openly angry with an employee? Yes _X_ No ___
   8a. Generally, for how long? _Momentarily._
9. At times is open anger the only way to handle a situation at work? Yes ___ No _X_
10. Think of the most miserable boss you've ever known.

Describe him or her. *Suspicious, mean, an ogre. He doesn't give you a chance.*

11. Do you think someone like that could become a nicer person? Yes _X_ No ___

12. If "yes," what would it take? *Someone doing the same thing to him. A tragedy that would bring him to his senses.*

13. Is anger part of the way things are in the company? Yes _X_ No ___

    13a. If "yes," what would it take to get that to change? *Fire my manager and get one with better people skills.*

Kathy: Let's look at your answers. What do they tell you?

Margaret: Well, I can see that when I'm dumped on, I dump on others. I know that. I don't feel anger is the only way, but how do I get around it?

Examining the Clues: What Margaret's Answers Mean

Kathy: Let's go farther and find out. I can compare your answers to hundreds of others we've analyzed. Overwhelmingly, anger spills over, just as it has with you. People get angry when they are frustrated, lose control, feel threatened, or are overwhelmed. Once the anger exists, it's hard to contain. For example, 95 percent of employees report that supervisors have become angry with them, 80 percent say it affects their work, and 75 percent report that they have become angry with their employees.

    The situations that make you angry—people not listening, disrespect, loss of control, arrogance, others not explaining problems—make others angry as well. You said that being on the receiving end of someone's anger makes you want to retaliate. Others have said things like they feel unworthy, small, belittled, frustrated, not wanting to go back to work.

    It's also clear that anger generally affects the quantity and quality of output. You've seen that in your case too.

We find that most people are very dramatic when describing their most miserable boss. Interestingly, though, these same people believe that their bosses could become nicer people.

Margaret: Well, most people might believe that, but I really don't. My boss can't change.

Kathy: The average person tends to be more generous, hopeful, and compassionate than the difficult people for whom he or she works. That's a clue for you right there. Can you approach your boss with generosity and compassion?

Let me help you. Here is a list of typical replies to question 12 about what it would take to get the miserable boss to change. Read them. Do you get any ideas?

To want to be better.
Be willing to share pressure and responsibility.
Remember to be human and recognize others' feelings.
Honesty and gain people's respect.
Behavior and attitude change.
Better listening skills.
More trust in people.
Time and improved communication.
Dialogue.
Relaxing.
Being honest and telling the person how his or her attitude and actions affect your work and home life.

Self-confidence and knowledge.
Counseling.
Peace with themselves.
Some serious psychotherapy.
Deep motivation such as from spouse, friend, or God.
Desire.
Treatment.
Bigger heart.
Opening up on a personal, in addition to a professional, level.
Profound enlightenment.
Something life threatening.

Margaret: What I see is that he has to feel better about himself, open up to others, and trust me so he can learn to deal with his anger.

Kathy: True, but remember that you're not his counselor. I want to help *you* handle your own distress and deal with him so that you feel in control. To do that, we need to explore your reactions to him. Close your eyes and imagine the face of your boss. Then answer these questions.

VISUALIZING THE ANGRY FACE

Imagine the face of the angry person in your life and answer these questions.

1. What is that person feeling? _____
2. Why do you think the person feels that way? ____
3. What do you feel when you look at that face? ____
4. Suppose you were that person's best friend. What would you be thinking? _____
5. Now imagine what you might say to your best friend. You've been asked for help. _____

Here are Margaret's responses to the questions shown in the box:

---

1. What is that person feeling? *I've got to get the jump on those people or they'll walk all over me.*
2. Why do you think that person feels that way? *He doesn't trust anybody. He's probably been taken advantage of.*
3. What do you feel when you look at that face? *He'll hurt me, or anyone else, to save himself. It's disgusting. He's scared. A little bit of pity.*
4. Suppose you were that person's best friend. What would you be thinking? *I'd almost cry. What can I do to help you? It must be awful.*
5. Now imagine what you might say to your best friend. You've been asked for help. *It isn't necessary for you to be so angry. See, I like you. I know many others who do,*

but they're just afraid to tell you. Would you like to talk about it?

Cracking the Case: How Margaret Can Tame Her Wild Boss

Kathy: Do you see what I've tried to do?

Margaret: Yes; you're trying to give me a different way of looking at him. But listen, I'm never going to become that guy's friend.

Kathy: You don't have to. I want to help you switch things around in your mind so you'll feel less trapped. Your emotional horizons, so to speak, will be broadened. You'll be better armed.

Margaret: Where do I go from here?

Kathy: Considering everything we've just talked about, complete each of the following sentences. Pretend that the "friend" is your boss. The finished sentences will tell you how you should approach your boss in the future.

Complete the following sentences:

1. My friend's behavior bothers me because _____.
2. If those difficult behaviors disappeared, my friend could _____.
3. I want to see my friend become _____.
4. Once my friend changed, then we could _____.
5. I'd like my friend even more, because _____.
6. If I ever became an angry person in the eyes of those I liked, I would hope _____.

Here are Margaret's responses to the sentence completion task shown in the box:

1. My friend's behavior bothers me because *he lessens my respect for myself.*
2. If those difficult behaviors disappeared, my friend could *make me want to come to work and do a good job.*
3. I want to see my friend become *more mature.*
4. Once my friend changed, then we could *work as a team.*
5. I'd like my friend even more, because *we could grow together.*
6. If I ever became an angry person in the eyes of those I liked, I would hope *people would tell me how I affect them.*

Margaret is a composite of many people, and she is trying to cope with one of the more distressing difficult behaviors in the workplace, an angry boss. The lessons from her experience could apply equally to coworkers as well as subordinates and people you know on or off the job.

The next week, Margaret called to report a number of incidents reflecting her progress at work. The conversation went something like this:

Margaret: He came up to me in the morning like he always does. This time I didn't remain seated. I jumped up and said, "I'm glad you're here. I was about to call you. I have an idea for simplifying this form. It might save us time and make our reports easier to follow." And I gave him a big smile.

Kathy: Sounds good to me. What did he do and say?

Margaret: He stood there. He didn't actually wilt, but he was overwhelmed. He had to smile. What else could he do? He wanted to study it. He never had a chance to get that mean look.

Kathy: You treated him like a friend?

Margaret: Not exactly. But it's getting close. The same sort of things happened on other days when I jumped the gun on him and offered him something. Sometimes it was just a smile and a few nice words.

Kathy: I'm really impressed and very pleased. I'm proud of you. Tell me how *you* felt.

Margaret: I felt good. I was in control, and I even began to feel sorry for the poor guy. He needs that attention. I think he gets angry when he yearns for something and

The out-of-control angry person needs to feel your inner strength. Therefore you cannot afford to be blown away. If you are the target and have truly made a mistake, admit it.

isn't getting it. At least that's my analysis. He doesn't frighten me. So I'm a better supervisor with my own people. Thanks. I owe you.

SOLUTIONS

What to Think

Following up on Margaret's insights, think this:

"The angry person is in trouble. The angry person could be, or could become, your friend."

Keep those two ideas in front of you at all times—when you are the target of abuse and insults, when you feel shut out, and when strong, irrational emotions seem to tie you in knots. But you will not lash back. Why? Because your own effectiveness will suffer, and you don't hurt people who need your help and who are in trouble. Never escalate anger.

What to Do

Take a deep breath and calm yourself, because you are not the cause of the outburst. Certainly you have your own feelings and don't like being picked on and demoralized, but you must be self-controlled and self-assured—the quiet spot in the eye of the storm. Picture this:

- Where the angry person's arms flail about, yours are at your sides.
- Where their face is twisted in a sneer, yours is relaxed.
- Where you see fists, your hands are open and signal acceptance.
- Where they yell, your voice is even and unhurried.

Never laugh, and walk out only if you think you may be in physical danger.

Depending on the circumstances, use or adapt one of the following phrases:

> "It's a rotten situation, but I think I know how to fix it."

> "I've felt exactly the way you have. I don't blame you. Tell me what you'd like me to do."

> "Yes, you're right. I'm going to review the whole thing and I'll have a recommendation [suggestion, solution] for you before the end of the day."

If the anger is generated by incidents or situations at work that do not involve you directly, your challenge is to provide an escape hatch. Phrases like, "You're right . . . I can't blame you . . . I'd feel the same way . . ." are helpful. The angry person needs an ally, and you can become one. In fact, times of crisis can help your career. Show your boss that he or she is in good, trusting hands and that your ability to defuse anger and restore calm can move the organization forward.

CHAPTER 2

SUSPICIOUS

Suspicion is the companion of mean souls.

—Thomas Paine

Ever watchful, suspicious people believe that others are ready to attack, hurt, or even kill them. They protect themselves to live another day by spreading seeds of doubt in the minds of others. But suspicion spawns suspicion, and they wonder what others know that they don't. They are fearful that if they miss something, they'll lose out. They imagine others as double agents and informants. There are no other alternatives.

THE CASE OF GEORGE AND THE MISTRUSTING MANAGER

"Hello, my name is George, I'm an engineer," says the big man, who looks successful and carries an expensive attaché case. He picks his words carefully and well.

"What I want to read to you are memos from my boss to his boss concerning my work. They think I'm going to jump ship with the company secrets, which are actually my own work." As he reads the memos, he makes comments: "Things are miserable. My department head is suspicious of me. He's just about convinced our manager of the same. Things are tough enough without having to worry about why people don't trust you anymore."

Bill: That's a terrible story. I can see you're agitated. Suspiciousness rubs off, especially if it comes down from the top.

George: I like my position and my field. I've been with my company ten years, and I like what I've created for my company. I want to save the situation, but how do I break through and get my superiors to trust me?

Bill: You've hit the problem on the head. It boils down to a question of trust. Would you mind answering some questions?

George: Anything, so long as it doesn't have to do with sex or politics.

We laughed. George sat down, breathed out slowly, and signaled that he was ready.

Bill: Do you believe that if you could learn to handle your department head's suspiciousness, you'd feel secure and satisfied in your job?

George: No question.

Bill: You will have to do the work required to accomplish that goal. Your department head isn't here, he will never be here, and you probably can't change him very much.

When one person, like yourself, alters how he or she treats another person, that person too may undergo a change in attitude. You might win in two ways: get better control of a situation you don't like and help your department head learn something positive.

So let's begin. On a scale of 1 to 5, 1 stands for extremely suspicious behavior, 2 for very suspicious, 3 for a realistic mix of doubt and trust, 4 for very trustful, and 5 for total trust. Think about your boss, and rate his behavior on the 1–5 scale for each quarter of the past two years.

George's responses are shown in Figure 1. Figure 2 contains a graph for you to fill out for your own suspicion rating of a difficult person.

Figure 1

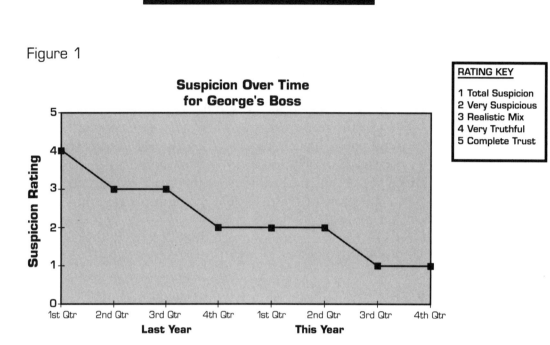

**Suspicion Over Time
for George's Boss**

RATING KEY

1 Total Suspicion
2 Very Suspicious
3 Realistic Mix
4 Very Truthful
5 Complete Trust

Figure 2

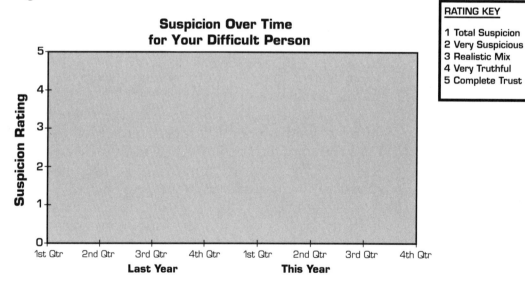

**Suspicion Over Time
for Your Difficult Person**

RATING KEY

1 Total Suspicion
2 Very Suspicious
3 Realistic Mix
4 Very Truthful
5 Complete Trust

George: Well, I can see that things have gotten much worse over time. His suspiciousness didn't really bother me until recently, though. I thought being a little paranoid came with his job as manager of engineering, but he's going too far.

Bill: A little paranoia may be necessary when you are protecting your company's patents and processes from the competition. But when you mistrust coworkers, it can sabotage their motivation.

George: That's certainly true. So my boss is the way he is, and he probably won't change much, right?

Bill: There's an outside chance that you could affect his behavior. But he's not here, you are; and he wouldn't think anything is wrong. Since you don't want to leave, you need to find techniques to get him to trust you more. Then you'll feel better. You have to step back and get a more objective look at your behavior. Complete each of the following sentences, and let's see what it tells us about your attitudes.

SUSPICIOUSNESS—UGH!

Complete the following sentences.

1. People who are suspicious make me feel _____.

2. When I think of a suspicious person I imagine ____.

3. Suspicious people are (list three):

   _____

   _____

   _____

4. A suspicious boss is _____.

5. Suspicion is harmful because it _____.

Here are George's responses to the sentence-completion exercise shown in the box. (Before you read them, fill out your own responses.)

1. People who are suspicious make me feel *guilty.*
2. When I think of a suspicious person I imagine *someone with a lot of power who can hurt other people.*
3. Suspicious people are (list three):
   Not happy people.
   Are sick.
   Might be smarter than the rest of us.
4. A suspicious boss is *someone I can't get out of my mind.*
5. Suspicion is harmful because it *kills trust and motivation.*

Examining the Clues: What George's Answers Mean

Bill: The elements you list include guilt, power, obsessive thoughts, and decreased motivation. Feeling guilt is your own hang-up. Assuming a suspicious person has the power to hurt you is also part of your attitude. George, all people don't react with guilt and fear as you do. Furthermore, you dwell on it, can't get it out of your mind. So, of course, as you say, your motivation is killed.

George: You're telling me I'm stuck, that it's a bad mix—poor chemistry between me and my boss.

Bill: Not quite. But you do have to inquire a little further into your attitudes. Now complete these sentences.

Research studies show that suspicious, mistrusting, and cynical people do not live as long as those who are not, even after taking into account age, smoking, alcohol use, and cholesterol level. In one

---

SUSPICIOUSNESS-UG-UGH!

Please complete the following brief questionnaire.

1. Suspicious people make me feel guilty because
   _____.

2. Suspicious people appear to have a lot of power because _____.

3. The way to get a suspicious person to trust you is _____.

study, test scores of suspiciousness clearly predicted the likelihood of a heart attack. Suspiciousness is unhealthy, say experts who study the connection between emotions and health.

Here are George's responses to the questions in the box:

1. Suspicious people make me feel guilty because *they pry and poke around, and who knows how they'll twist things.*
2. Suspicious people appear to have a lot of power because *they act as if they are the guardians of value and virtue, and the rest of us can't be trusted.*
3. The way to get a suspicious person to trust you is *to admit to everything, but that may not last too long either.*

Cracking the Case: How George Can Build a Bridge of Trust to His Boss

Bill: Okay, George. Look at your answers, and suggest a plan of action.

George: I see two things that I have to deal with. First, my boss never feels that he knows everything that is happening. He thinks people are hiding things. Maybe I need to give him every bit of information available to me. Write lots of memos and provide him with heaps of data. Tell him everything I'm doing. He needs quantity almost more than quality.

Second, he triggers guilt and fear inside me. But I have nothing to feel guilty about, and knowing all that I've contributed to the company, I should have nothing to fear. It's up to me to control those feelings. It's my problem, not his. I won't let him do it to me anymore.

I pity the poor guy. He's unhappy and looks it. I also know that he can be a danger to unsuspecting people.

George's boss is chronically suspicious. If George can make a dent, ignite even the smallest spark of trust, he will be performing a decent and humane deed. George's motivation? To save his self-esteem and protect the meaning of his job. Here are George's significant realizations:

- Suspicious people are never satisfied (history attests to that point).
- Suspicious people can be warded off for a time with quantities of information.
- Suspicion produces a climate of self-doubt; it is an attack on your integrity. George asked why he should feel guilty. He found no reason. He asked himself if he should be fearful. And again it proved to be groundless.

Now we'll take the lessons in George's story and apply them.

SOLUTIONS

What to Think

The suspicious person always needs a target—a victim. Suspicion can't go anywhere or do anything—cannot be satisfied—unless it attaches to someone or some group. The probabilities of your being correctly blamed (targeted), however, are very small. In other words, think:

"I am almost always without guilt."

At work, you can seldom leave the scene and walk out. The suspicious boss, team leader, or coworker must be dealt with. You find your motives being questioned and your behavior placed under a microscope. Say to yourself and think:

"I'm not a bug to be played with. My motives are pure, my behavior good."

Say, as George did,

"I pity the guy."

What to Do

You can successfully confront suspicion only with your ego intact and your self-esteem high. The weak and fearful are easy marks. Don't become one.

You must disentangle yourself from the suspicious person's web. You must say,

"I don't belong there; I've done nothing wrong."

What you must *never* do, however, is pass suspicion down. Suspicion does breed more of the same, so if it starts with you, stop the process right there.

Watch yourself carefully. Watch for those "crazy thoughts" about others; they are often subtle and insidious. Suspicion can't grow in sunlight and truth. Therefore, once you begin to feel the virus of severe doubt and suspicion start to affect your ideas about friends and coworkers, seek help—not necessarily professional help but help from a friend. Open dialogue will clear your mind and chase away the shadows.

Finally, do not believe anything the suspicious person says about you, either to your face or behind your back.

Say your boss accuses you of a late report that you misplaced. You know it hasn't been misplaced, nor is it late. To prove you are guiltless, refer to the documentation and memos: "According to this note [memo, fax, etc.] the report was due on June 3, and I sent it to Paul, just as I was instructed to do." Don't make the encounter into a contest because you will seldom win. Don't get upset or defensive either. Don't let the old guilts—things that may bother all of us from time to time—surface and get in the way. Treat the situation in as matter-of-fact a way as you can. *Don't get caught in the web!*

Say you're accused of not doing your work as well as you should—in other words, of becoming a failure in your leader's eyes. You're being watched. The story is spread around that you're not working well. How do you handle your boss, and how do you stop the rumors? How, quite possibly, do you protect your career?

Your boss? Remember one rule: truth and sunshine. Present

the facts, document them, and make the presentation; be calm, pleasant, and nonthreatening. Don't become cowed. Suspicious bosses go after people who appear vulnerable and yield to them, and ultimately they become their accomplice in spreading suspicion. It is absolutely necessary that you enter that war zone with the solid personal conviction that you are guiltless.

Your coworkers? Some will be strong and some weak. The weak ones will assume you are guilty; the strong ones will wait to see how you do in handling the boss. Once it's discovered—and it will be—that you cannot be intimidated and targeted, you'll find yourself with increased informal authority. You will be left alone. Sometimes an amazing thing will happen: Your career prospects will improve in the eyes of your boss's managers because you'll become defined as a strong person.

CHAPTER 3

PESSIMISTS

Do you know what a pessimist is? A man who thinks everybody is as nasty as himself, and hates them for it.

—George Bernard Shaw

Pessimists speak our own unspeakable fears—fears so overwhelming that when we hear the words, we laugh, thinking it is the pessimist we are laughing at, when in truth we are denying our own anxieties.

In the movies the pessimist always gets a big laugh, but if you work with someone full of doom and gloom, you're probably not laughing. The pessimist demands your time, drains your energy, and clouds your critical judgment. Why the difference between the pessimist in the arts and literature and in real life? Why do these people who expect the worst to happen, who cry when others laugh, and who search for the dark side strike our funny bone? One reason is that we feel pessimists can't hurt us. They are harmless, weak, and to be pitied. We reach out to them with compassion—"There, there, it can't be that bad." They are like frightened, foolish children, to be taken seriously only up to a point.

It makes some people feel good to compare themselves to the pessimist. Life confronts us with a question like, "What's the worst that can happen?" And we answer, "Nothing, not to me, but to the pessimists everything goes wrong. They ask for it." But a little bit of pessimism in an environment filled with crazy, cockeyed optimists can be a good thing.

THE CASE OF RON AND THE GLOOMY GROUP LEADERS

Ron, a large, artfully balanced man of fifty, introduces himself as a machinist. He is polite, pleasant, and calm. His company produes high-precision components for the computer and medical industries. He oozes confidence and seems quite capable. We had been able to pick up some of the stress in other people who had come to see us. Ron seemed different. What could he possibly be concerned about?

Ron: I've come about my team. There are seven of us, all equal, and once a month we rotate into the leader's position. This month, it's me again, so it'll be all right. My problem is two of the team members. When it's their turn to be team leaders, the whole group goes sour. We manage to get out the work—most of the work, I should say—but we're all down. It's a strain, like working in low gear.

Kathy: That's a great description. What do you think is wrong?

Ron: I don't know how much you know about my field— tool and die people, machinists. We're not by nature the most optimistic people in the world. We're careful and believe only in what we can see and touch. That doesn't mean we're pessimists either.

Kathy: Do you mean two of your members are pessimists, and that's why the group goes sour?

Ron: I know they are pessimists. To them everything is going to go wrong. They believe that jobs will never be done on time, mistakes will be too late to be corrected, and someone's always bound to make a mistake. They are doom and gloom. I know their effect on us is bad. It rubs off. During the months they're team leaders, I come home feeling sad myself. Why is that? I didn't realize what they were doing to me until my wife mentioned something. She thought I was sick. Pessimism is contagious.

Kathy: Do they have reason to be pessimistic? Don't they like their jobs? The company's prospects? How about their health? Is there something you may not be aware of?

Ron: No, they are young, in good health. They're very good at what they do. Once I thought about it, I realized that they have always been this way. In the past, however, it wasn't so noticeable because we all worked pretty much alone. Since we've begun working in teams, their pessimism has become more obvious.

Kathy: It's clear what you're describing. Pessimism affects everything it touches. But what do you have in mind? Do you have a plan of your own?

Ron: I do. I'm convinced that the way to get around the pessimism is the way it appeared in the first place: within the team. I want to involve the whole team. Can you help? It won't be practical to bring the whole team here.

An individual's negative emotions on a team—pessimism is one example—can impede the group process. Remedies can focus on the individual or be directed toward the group itself. The solution recommended for Ron will be through the group. Situations of truly destructive behavior, however, such as out-of-control hostility, hyperactivity, or extreme withdrawal, can require professional help.

Kathy: No need for that. You can lead the effort to attack this problem for your team. Are you willing to be the group facilitator? That means you'll encourage people to express themselves, to be tactful and supportive, and avoid blame. You will have to explain that the discussion of feelings and attitudes, based on the questionnaires I'll give you, is to help the team function better.

Ron: I have to do it.

Kathy: Okay, here's a true/false questionnaire [see the box] that focuses on feelings and pessimism. Have your team members complete the forms and discuss the answers in the group. I'm not concerned with how deep-seated someone's pessimism may be, nor should you be. Permit the group to come to its own conclusion as to what's acceptable or not when they meet as a team. You'll see that pessimistic behavior will not be acceptable.

We've indicated what we feel to be the preferred answers and explain why. Use those answers merely as starting points for discussion. Explain that their own answers are neither wrong nor right.

TEAM CLIMATE QUESTIONNAIRE

1. The difference between an optimist and a pessimist is merely one of degree.   T   F
2. So long as I do my work, my coworkers have no right to get involved in my feelings.   T   F
3. Enthusiasm is contagious.   T   F
4. Pessimism is contagious.   T   F
5. There is something that can be called a team personality.   T   F
6. A team's personality can be affected by its leader.   T   F
7. Energetic, proactive teams can accomplish more than laid-back, pessimistic ones.   T   F
8. Things always go wrong whether you want them to or not—Murphy's Law—so why fight it.   T   F
9. The team idea is just a clever way to get us to work more for the same rewards.   T   F
10. Team members don't really care about one another; they just say it because they think they should.   T   F

As in many of these irritating, difficult person interchanges, the primary goal is helping the person who has to deal with the problem. Deep-seated pessimism is seldom amenable to dramatic changes using a counseling or therapy model but can be modified within a group context.

EXAMINING THE CLUES: WHAT THE ANSWERS MEAN

1. *False.* They are different kinds of personalities, and seldom can one turn into the other, even though most people can experience both kinds of feelings.
2. *False.* Feelings (emotions) have powerful influences on productivity and quality. Within a team those influences are even stronger.
3. *True.* Energy and high performance can be infused into a group by the optimism of a few key people. We see it every day.
4. *True.* The naysayers and predictors of doom can spark and magnify the small bit of uncertainty in all of us.
5. *True.* It's a reality. Research studies have confirmed that teams have a personality. They share beliefs and establish rules of the game. They may be enthusiastic or solemn, all related to the mix of people, their leaders, and the group's goals.
6. *True.* Any leader can affect the mood of the team, whether in a company, sports, or even a country. Leaders influence productivity and morale.
7. *True.* Energy drives activity, which leads to effective problem solving.
8. *False.* Murphy's Law is the pessimist's invention. It's funny but not true.
9. *False.* Teams are supposed to help employees work smarter and quicker, and discover better procedures and processes. Teams should enable you to produce more with the same input while learning new skills and protecting your future.
10. *False.* The sense of trust and friendship created within any team or group, whether in industry, education, religion, or athletics, is a powerful force for cooperation and effort.

Cracking the Case: How Ron Can Get His Team Out of the Dumps

Kathy: After your team has discussed the answers to the true/false quiz, have them fill out this next form [see the box titled "The Pessimist's and Optimist's Reactions," which is an exercise and a rehearsal for less pessimistic behavior. Please be careful not to point out your two pessimists. Everyone knows who they are, and it's better left unsaid. Once the team completes these forms, discuss them as a group. There aren't any right or wrong answers. This exercise does two things: it helps the group look at the problem without putting anyone on the defensive, and it makes clear the difference between the way pessimists and optimists see things.

Ron: Do you actually think these methods of yours will turn those guys around?

Kathy: If you mean will they suddenly become optimists, probably not. But they will be influenced to conform to the degree of optimism or pessimism acceptable to the group. You're not looking for the heat of summer or the ice of winter but rather the springtime of conciliation and teamwork.

The pessimist who works alone may irritate coworkers, who can simply learn to avoid that person. That kind of easy solution, avoidance, isn't possible within a work group. Think of teams that are effective and produc-

If you must deal with a pessimistic coworker in a one-on-one situation, the techniques for handling this irritating behavior are different from the methods for a team situation. It is important to examine how the pessimistic behavior affects you. Try to look at the pessimistic person more objectively. The best technique for diffusing the pessimist in a nonteam environment involves fighting fire with fire. Try an in-your-face countermaneuver: doing what the pessimist is doing to you, a technique described in detail in the next chapter.

tive. In those groups, positive qualities like optimism, mutual dependence, trust, and support are reinforced. Negative qualities like pessimism, extreme competitiveness, or cynicism are not tolerated.

THE PESSIMIST'S AND OPTIMIST'S REACTIONS

Read each statement, and then describe how you feel a pessimist and an optimist would react to each situation.

1. Your supervisor says, "If we all work on this final step in the process, we can get out of here by five and get the order out on time."

   The optimist thinks _____

   The pessimist thinks _____

2. A coworker tells a friend that he's heard that next week will see the end of overtime. New people are being hired.

   The optimist thinks _____

   The pessimist thinks _____

3. A team leader says that rewards for any new techniques developed by the group will be shared equally.

   The optimist thinks _____

   The pessimist thinks _____

4. Management announces that it doesn't plan to relocate the plant.

   The optimist thinks _____

   The pessimist thinks _____

5. The team leader says that it is important that people trust one another and if someone has a good idea to share it with the group.

   The optimist thinks _____

   The pessimist thinks _____

SOLUTIONS

What to Think

Pessimists cannot be dismissed lightly. Their outlook on life will make you less vigilant and lull you into accepting mediocre performance. Do not permit yourself to be seduced by the pessimist's point of view.

If a pessimist works for you, think this:

> "Is it [the project, report, projection, field situation] really that bad? What information could have been left out or disregarded? Is the timetable correct?"

Then be aware that the pessimist is going to lower your standards, and you can't let that happen.

If you are a team leader, and a pessimist is a member of your team, as in Ron's case, watch out for two possible outcomes: decreases in group performance and a decrease in your usual level of enthusiasm and energy. If you see that happening, think this:

> "I'm getting contaminated; I'm being compromised. I must use the power of the team to help myself and the team."

What to Do

It's important to distinguish pessimists from employees who are lazy, sloppy, or just plain incompetent. How do you tell the difference? Here are some clues. People who are lazy, sloppy, or incompetent are generally known quantities to coworkers. They tend to provoke, annoy, and anger others. Pessimists, on the other hand, are usually acceptable. But their effects are subtle because you think they can't harm you.

Every organization has its own hot-button issues around which people have strong positive or negative feelings. The five set out in the box on pessimists' and optimists' reactions are general. Important group issues for your team may include concerns about diversity,

sharing bonuses and rewards, sexual harassment, or performance reviews. We recommend that you take this format and develop statements that will reflect your company. Use these if you wish, but it's best to tailor-make the items now that you know the method.

Recognizing a pessimist is the vital first step. They can masquerade as cautious, careful, and conservative employees, and you may never know they are pessimists at heart. For example, suppose a chain of departments must handle a project, passing information from one level to the next. You are a manager, studying that process, watching for blips, trying to make the system more efficient. Time and again, you discover, information gets stuck in the same department and the smooth flow is interrupted. You might think, "They're being careful. It pays at times not to rush things." Suppose next that you stumble across this book or a professional article about pessimism. "Can it be," you muse, "that I've overlooked something?" Our advice? Get out there, and see if you have a pessimist masquerading as a careful, conscientious employee.

Once you've found your pessimist, you'll see it's not a stupid or lazy employee but quite the contrary: a loyal, skilled, and good employee. Still, you can't afford to slow down the process of work. What do you do?

Put the pessimist at the end of the process, where worrying and extra caution can pay off. Pessimists can be good watchdogs. They'll look for trouble and errors where there may be none, but if errors are present, they'll find them where no one else might.

If tasks can be shared, pair the pessimist with an energetic employee and hope that a friendship develops. It's astounding what shared responsibility can accomplish.

If the pessimist is highly skilled—and many are—assign solo tasks and projects where careful analysis is more important than quick response.

If the pessimist is a member of a team, returning to Ron's story, you are lucky, because the team will solve the problem by following our recommendations.

CHAPTER 4

CYNICS

What is a cynic? A man who knows the price of everything and the value of nothing.

—Oscar Wilde

The cynic questions everything. There is some value in questioning things. After all, only the very naive and gullible believe everything they hear. But if you question everything, what's left to believe?

A cynic is distrustful of human nature and motives. Suspicion, pessimism, and selfishness are all part of it, but a true cynic brings something more to the party. A true cynic will challenge your belief in what you hold most dear. President Franklin Roosevelt expressed it well when he said, "Those cynical men who say that democracy cannot be honest and efficient." He did not say, "those suspicious, pessimistic, selfish men."

They can sound so clever, those cynical friends of ours. During your first week at a new job, they point out that orientation is a joke run by corporate cheerleaders. They smirk when you volunteer for a Community Chest drive. When sales bonuses are announced, you'll hear, "Don't get your hopes up because they won't do it [give the bonuses]."

The cynic will say, "Nothing—and it's about time you found out. Look out for number one."

As with all other negative behavior, cynical attitudes are contagious. They creep into a workplace and gradually undermine enthusiasm and confidence. And in today's workplace, where trust and loyalty are in short supply, cynicism falls on fertile ground.

THE CASE OF RED AND THE DOUBTING MANAGER

The young man who walks in next is alive with energy. "I'm Red!" he shouts. "That's my nickname." But he didn't have to explain. Red is very tall and thin, and his hair is indeed red, as are his freckles and even his tie. He is a salesman and is "doing very well." "I'm a perennial optimist," he explains. "I do my homework, I move, I sell." It's true; Red's enthusiasm brightens the day.

Red: Let me tell you why I'm here. Don't laugh; it's serious to me. It's my friend and marketing manager. I should say my almost ex-friend. He's a pathological cynic, if that's the right phrase. His remarks used to seem funny to me. He's clever, can stand things on their heads, and get you to see things you never thought of. But when he's through with tearing something apart, I feel drained, and it's like carrying a big stone around my neck. There's nothing left. I lose my drive. It's as if he's reached inside me and found the circuit breaker that turns me on and off. The way you're seeing me, I'm *on* now, but there are many days when I'm in the *off* position.

Bill: What's the worst thing that could happen to you in the future as a result of your cynical manager's influence?

Red: That hanging around him will turn me off completely. That I won't be able to sell.

Bill: You wouldn't recognize yourself. But you know what he's like, so why are you so affected by his cynicism?

Red: Hey, if I knew the answer to that one, I wouldn't be here. I know I'm beginning to lose my edge. You're going to have to help me find the answer. I'll do anything.

Bill: I'll try. There is one thing you should know: Cynicism, like anger, suspicion, and extreme competitiveness, falls into a gray area. They're almost acceptable nowadays. Watch your TV; it's popular.

Red: You mean, a little bit's all right, but a lot will make you sick?

Bill: Right. What the cynic lacks is a plan to put things together after he takes something apart. It is important to be streetwise. And if you take everything at face value, you'll surely be stepped on and passed over. The problem with your manager friend is that he has moved from healthy skepticism to complete cynicism.

I want to find out how you feel when you interact with your manager. Complete the sentences [see the box] with the first thoughts that come to mind.

KNOW YOUR CYNIC QUESTIONNAIRE

Complete the following sentences.

1. I enjoy listening to a cynic when _____.

2. There are times when the cynic makes me feel _____.

3. I could never be a true cynic for these three reasons:

   _____

   _____

   _____

4. I can't really trust a cynic because _____.

5. A cynic doesn't believe what he or she is told because _____.

Here are Red's responses:

---

1. I enjoy listening to a cynic when *I'm angry and annoyed about something.*

2. There are times when the cynic makes me feel *scared.*
3. I could never be a true cynic for these three reasons:
   People wouldn't like me.
   I wouldn't want to see the world in such negatives terms.
   My career could eventually be hurt.
4. I can't really trust a cynic because *I don't think he believes in anything.*
5. A cynic doesn't believe what he or she is told because *they mistrust the intentions of others.*

Examining the Clues: What Red's Answers Mean

Bill: Your response to question 1 isn't surprising. Cynics speak openly about what others feel when they are frustrated and upset—in your words, "angry and annoyed." The times when you're upset, you will be drawn to your friend. Then he's a hero because he's unafraid to say aloud what you feel. You can use that positive reaction as a barometer for your own feelings. You might be angry and frustrated and not know it. Then you run into your manager and like what you hear. When you're on top of things and feeling good, the cynic's remarks lose their appeal. That explains your answer to question 2. The cynic can be scary to others because nothing is sacred. Nothing has any solid meaning. When you hear him laugh at life, it can shake you if he's contradicting your beliefs and values.

Red: I'm getting more than I bargained for, but please go on.

Bill: You're writing your own analysis of a cynic and it's good. In question 3 you point out the consequences of being negative. You could be rejected by people important to you—coworkers as well as friends. Your career might even suffer. That's a big insight.

I'm going to suggest that you don't want to be rejected and your career derailed because, as you said at the very beginning, you're a perennial optimist and you

In my experience, and in the judgment of counselors and other behavioral scientists, when someone doesn't trust others, they have problems trusting themselves as well.

want an edge. Cynicism is against your nature. Being as negative as your manager might make you a less-than-desirable candidate for promotion in the eyes of the big bosses.

The core of the problem, as you see it, is that you believe your manager doesn't trust others. You're a salesman and know what I mean. If it ever got to the point where you lost trust in and had doubts about your product, you'd be in pretty sad shape.

Red: All well and good. Right on the mark. You educated me. Now how do I handle the guy?

Cracking the Case: How Red Keeps His Positive Attitude

Bill: You've already come a long way toward handling him. You just need a method to use. It's called Disarming by Exaggeration. This is how it works. You can neutralize the negative effects of the cynic's remarks on yourself by purposely outdoing him—being more cynical than he is—while retaining whatever insights they may contain. You strike me as a good actor. You can do it.

Red: I am a good actor. It's one reason I'm successful. But let me get this straight. I go him one better on purpose, like I'm burlesquing him to his face, only he doesn't know I'm imitating him. Is that what you mean by Disarming by Exaggeration? You know—I've done that as a joke, now that you mention it. I have no problem with the method, but tell me again how that will help me overcome his negative influence.

Bill: First, as you've already found out, it isn't difficult to be cynical if you want to. The mystery of it will be reduced like this: If he can do it and you can do it, what's the big deal? Second, in your own mind, you've made it into a contest, a game—something like two kids hurling insults at one another. A game isn't real life. Do you know what I mean when I say you will have pulled his teeth?

Red: I sure do. The sting is gone. Let me at him! I'm ready to go. Where is he?

Bill: I believe you are ready. But before you dash off let's try rehearsing. Let's say the cynic told you, "They say they are going to hire more people to help with the influx of new business. If you believe that you'll believe that elephants can fly." How would you reply?

Red: Let me think. Okay. Here's what I would say: "I know. I heard they were going to put bunk beds and showers in the basement, so we could work sixteen hours a day without ever going home." How's that?

REHEARSALS FOR REPLYING TO A CYNIC

What does your *cynic* say?
What do *you* say?

1. *Cynic:* _____

   You: _____

2. *Cynic:* _____

   You: _____

3. *Cynic:* _____

   You: _____

SOLUTIONS

What to Think

Red's case gives you a baseline for handling cynics. We'll summarize them. Think:

> "A cynic will dull my competitive edge. A cynic doesn't believe in anything. It's not difficult to imitate what a cynic does."

There is more you should know: Cynicism negatively affects morale, especially if it comes down from your boss. Co-workers are far easier to handle. Think:

> "I don't know what the game is but for some reason our boss is causing us all to perform at a lower level than we can."

Think again:

> "I must be careful. Our boss can now pick off any one of us, claiming less than acceptable perform-ance."

This last insight is what Red was talking about when he mentioned losing his edge, and his "switch" being in the "off" position.

Once you recognize that career protection and self-defense is your objective, your behavior will become focused, and you will be able to avoid the verbal traps of the cynic.

What to Do

It is very easy to become cynical about life, work, and the government. TV sound bites and newspaper headlines fuel doubt and skepticism. "Do we ever hear the truth?" we wonder. "Can anyone be trusted?"

You have to control your own situations. Don't let the cynic contaminate and demoralize you. Protecting yourself begins with the thoughts above. In addition to Disarming by Exaggeration there are a few more tricks you can use to insulate yourself:

1. You are home and without warning spring cynical comments—humorous if possible—on your family and friends. They may think you're weird, which is fine. Then tell them about your workplace cynic and encourage them to tell you about *their* experiences. Talking about your difficult person at work will loosen their effect on you at the office.
2. Get yourself some joke books and look for the cyni-

cal examples; they're always there. Memorize a few and tell them at work. Urge others to do the same. What will happen? Cynicism itself will eventually become the joke of the office.

3. Become the scholar and student. (This is the reasonable man or woman approach.) Arm yourself with substantiated facts to counter the cynic's typically grand condemnations. Remember to smile.

CHAPTER 5

SHY AND QUIET

Fear of danger is ten thousand times more terrifying than danger itself.

—Daniel Defoe, *Robinson Crusoe*

What evil lurks in the hearts of men and women? That's the reaction of others to people who keep to themselves and don't share feelings of joy, sadness, love, or hate. They may simply be shy, quiet, or timid, but the message "Leave me alone!" goes out to coworkers. "You touch me (my feelings) and break my wall, you pay." Coworkers think, "He's up to something sneaky," "She's such a snob," or "He's antisocial; he must really hate all of us." So people stay away from that quiet person, not knowing what to do. But these quiet people don't give their behavior a thought and are usually unaware of their effect on the office atmosphere.

THE CASE OF FRED AND THE SILENT SUPERVISOR

Fred bounces into the room, full of energy, looking like your favorite Sunday afternoon quarterback. You have to like him; he wouldn't have it any other way. When he speaks, his unruly blond hair seems to stand straight up on his head. He said he had to come. His problem was driving him crazy.

Fred: I was recently promoted to manager, and I *must* succeed. No one's ever been promoted to this job at my age. My problem is Janet, one of the supervisors on my staff. She seems like a good worker but won't talk to me. Of course, she doesn't talk to anyone else either.

She just comes to work, does her job, and asks that people don't bother her. But if someone needs help, she's very patient and instructs them. The problem is, our productivity has been slipping lately. I think part of it is that everyone in the department walks on eggshells around Janet. They're hesitant to approach her, and it disrupts the work flow. The added tension also distracts some of the staff members from their work. Maybe she's afraid of something or just hates me.

I don't know what to do. Sometimes I just sit and stare into the distance trying to find the key to unlock Janet's distant look. When I feel my own mood growing cold, I get scared and quickly put on my usual handsome smile. I like to bring every issue out on the table. Growing up, my family always talked about a problem and solved it together. I just don't think that approach will work with Janet. It's getting to the point where I am afraid to approach her. Boy, do I need help.

Bill: Well, what really bothers you most about Janet's behavior? Is it just that she is unfriendly, or is there a problem with her work?

Fred: Tension is high, productivity is slipping, and Janet's the reason. I don't think she's aware of the way people feel about her and of the tension she generates.

Bill: To solve this problem you need to begin by exploring your feelings about people like Janet. Let's start by having you fill out this questionnaire [see the box].

SHYNESS ANALYSIS FORM

Complete the following questionnaire.

1. Withdrawn people bother me because _____
2. How do quiet people feel about others? _____
3. Rank from 1 to 5 the following reasons that shy and quiet people keep others away (1 is the most important and 5 is the least important).

They are afraid of people. ___
They don't like people. ___
They've done something they are ashamed
   of. ___
They are afraid they'll be hurt again. ___
If they open up, they'll be ridiculed. ___

4. I can't imagine ever being a quiet, withdrawn
    person because _____

5. I find it harder to trust a quiet person than some-
    one who is outgoing and friendly.
       Yes ___ No ___ Sometimes ___

Here are Fred's responses:

---

1. Withdrawn people bother me because *they are thinking
    things about me that are probably negative.*
2. How do quiet people feel about others? *They laugh at
    other people and think they are better than everyone
    else.*
3. Rank from 1 to 5 the following reasons that shy and
    quiet people keep others away (1 is the most important
    and 5 is the least important).
       They are afraid of people. _4_
       They don't like people. _1_
       They've done something they are ashamed of. _3_
       They are afraid they'll be hurt again. _5_
       If they open up, they'll be ridiculed. _2_
4. I can't imagine ever being a quiet, withdrawn person be-
    cause *if I couldn't interact with others, I'd be lost and
    miserable.*
5. I find it harder to trust a quiet person than someone
    who is outgoing and friendly. Yes_X_ No ___ Some-
    times ___

Examining the Clues: What Fred's Answers Mean

Bill: Fred, you assume because your supervisor is quiet, her thoughts are negative and she knows things she's not revealing. You think she's laughing at others. You can't trust such a person. On the other hand, your answers to question 3 reveal some compassion and a feeling that the quiet person may have been hurt in her own life.

You can't conceive of being quiet and withdrawn, because interacting with others is what makes your life meaningful. Except for that touch of compassion, you can't possibly identify with Janet. There's an emotional gulf between the two of you.

What would you like to say to Janet if you could say *anything* you wished?

Fred: "Janet, you're making it impossible for me to work with you. Maybe you're not aware of it, but you are too damn quiet for me. I want to help you enjoy what you are doing and become a more active member of this department."

Bill: What do you imagine she might say?

Fred: "Leave me alone Fred. I'm not here to have a good time. I could care less that you want to be my buddy and want everyone to be happy. I do my job, isn't that enough for you? Grow up, you worm."

Bill: Pretty funny—and maybe a little tragic. It seems as if you are being too tough on yourself. She's a difficult person to handle, and you're running scared. You imagine that if you can't solve the puzzle of Janet, you won't be a successful manager. Does that make sense?

Fred: Too much sense. I admit that I am a little insecure. But I'd still like to know exactly what to do and say. I have to succeed.

Bill: Try this approach: Sit down with her in your office, forget the stare, and say, "I know we haven't gotten along well. How about starting over again?" She may laugh, but you're big enough to be laughed at. Remember, you need to open the communication lines

Communicating and dealing with a withdrawn or very quiet person is a difficult experience for a co-worker, manager, or team leader. Fred's responses to the questionnaire indicate why: fear of the unknown. Loners are often shaking inwardly, afraid to interact with others. Meanwhile their coworkers are creating unrealistic ideas about them.

and get her to talk. Make small wins. You say, smiling, "How about saying 'hello' to each other in the morning, or saying, 'see you tomorrow at the end of the day'?" Small steps are what it's all about—building a work life vocabulary together.

Fred: I think I can do that. First I forget the stare; it's not aimed at me, I know that. Then we begin to talk; the subject's not that important. Just build a work life together that works.

Bill: Now that we've agreed, let's rehearse. I'll be you and you play Janet. It's going to be easier than you think.

With some insight into his reactions to Janet, Fred is ready as the nonquiet person to make the first move.

What do shy, quiet people want? Mostly, to participate on their own terms—slowly, without being pushed, while being given an opportunity to make a meaningful contribution. Fred can use department-wide conferences and assignments to help his quiet supervisor open up to others.

Cracking the Case: How Fred Can Bring Janet Out of Her Shell

Bill: Now let's try a rehearsal. I'll play you. You be Janet and say what you think she might say, whatever it is.
Fred: Let's rock 'n' roll.

This is how the rehearsal went. Bill is now playing Janet's role:

Fred: Janet I want to let you know I've decided to begin a series of department meetings. I've been thinking a lot about how to motivate people—help them work together and reach their best potential.
Janet: [10-second pause] Yes?
Fred: Well, what I meant to say was that these meetings shouldn't be run by me. I am the manager, but I believe that everyone in our group should learn how to manage and lead. What do you think?

Janet: [8-second pause] You want us to work more closely together? To be a team?

Fred: That's right, but more than that really. I think everyone should get a chance to run some of the meetings and share leadership.

Janet: [5-second pause] I know what you mean, I'm not stupid, you know. You want me to get up there in front of the group. No way! I'd rather die . . .

Many timid people do have a sense of humor about their walled-off personalities, as if to say, "Catch me if you can." They will absolutely *not* want to handle a group. They probably will be willing to sit in with the group. A persuasive and perceptive leader and the natural dynamics of the group will help the timid person out of his or her emotional corner.

Such an approach usually works because of these reasons:

- Members learn to trust one another through working together toward a united goal.
- Members take pleasure in the growth and attainments of others.
- The group becomes supportive of its members.
- The group creates a new energy of its own that the timid person absorbs, enabling him or her to interact more openly.

SOLUTIONS

What to Think

Put yourself in that person's shoes. This is what it can sound like inside their heads: "Those people out there are different from me. What's wrong? I want to be like them—talking, joking, laughing, saying what I wish. I hate myself for being different. Why can't someone see it?" Think:

> "If I were a shy person, I'd pray for someone to reach in, help me, and not scare me."

The most important thing to remember is that shy, quiet people do not dislike you, and they are not harboring or hatching secret negative plans.

Even Fred, as ambitious as he is, feels a little bit of compassion. But he's so wrapped up in his own career that Janet is someone to get out of the way rather than a colleague who needs help.

What to Do

Use a group environment to draw silent colleagues out of their shells. Encourage withdrawn staff members to join organizations like Toastmasters or Dale Carnegie. If, unlike Fred, you have a trusting relationship with a coworker who has trouble interacting with others, offer to help that person rehearse more assertive behavior.

To rehearse better behavior, the first step is that the distant person has to admit there is a problem. If you are a friend, you can tactfully talk about offering help. If you are a coworker, you can bring up the problem by talking about careers in general. There has to be trust. And it always helps if you genuinely like the other person.

Consider this example. Your project partner and friend, Steve, is timid. He knows what he's doing, but when a customer comes through and asks a question, he responds with a blank stare, and his face turns gray. You've learned not to leave him alone, so you jump in and "save it." What to do? Prep him. That means you rehearse him: You're the customer, Steve is you. He'll fumble at first. No problem. Then let him "imitate" himself, then you, back and forth. Finally suggest that Steve be the customer, then you be him, then yourself, back and forth. After a few sessions, the whole experience of timidity in front of customers will be materially reduced. And you will have given your partner a true gift. His timidity in general will be lessened. Isn't that something great to do for a friend?

CHAPTER 6

HOW DO I LOVE ME?

I dote on myself, there is that lot of me and all so luscious.

—Walt Whitman

How dull life would be without our narcissists. Who would be there to demand our attention, distract us from our own concerns and priorities, and compel us to dance to their tune?

"What, you didn't notice me come into the room—me? You don't know what you missed." So thinks the adored one, the gift-to-the-world entertainer, athlete, leader, subordinate, or coworker.

THE CASE OF GRACE AND THE OFFICE PRINCESS

The woman who walks in could play the role of the all-knowing, all-understanding aunt in your favorite soap. She is a self-composed person whose smile is synchronized to her movements. As she extends her arm to make a point or leans forward to emphasize a phrase, her mouth forms an arc and her eyes brighten. Her name is Grace; she's a department manager in an insurance company. Grace is married; after raising five children, she returned to work. Her first words are, "Spare me the beautiful people."

She needs no prompting. All we have to do is smile and nod.

Grace: There are eleven young people in my department, nice men and women. And then there's Michelle Madonna. At least that's what we call her. Michelle loves Michelle, which could be acceptable if she saved her narcissism for after work. But she's driving me crazy. My department's a family, and Michelle is my spoiled brat.

I suppose I should have known better when I hired her, but—as I'm sure you know—people like that can be real charmers—everybody's darling and favorite. Now it's too late, and I have no one to blame but myself. But her work's passable, and she can learn quickly when she wants to. Worst of all, she's made friends with some of the people over me, and heaven knows what she's saying. She's my problem—Michelle Madonna. What do I do?

Bill: You've come to one conclusion. You don't want her to destroy your department or your reputation. From what you've said, so far the game's been played by her rules, so it isn't going to be easy to get her to change. To do that, everyone has to respond to her differently than they do now.

People like Michelle can't conceive of the possibility of someone's not liking and wanting them. Most of your staff see through her, but it's doubtful that they've been able to do much about changing things.

Grace: It isn't so much me. I'm thinking of the rest of the group. Michelle's effect—it's not easy to describe—crept up on us. I've watched the transition over six months. She went from a charming, friendly coworker to a spoiled brat, demanding and getting everyone's time and attention. It sounds strange. Can you understand how that happened?

Bill: It's not strange at all. It works this way. The narcissist disarms you with an endearing quality. You identify with part of it. We all see a tiny bit of ourselves in the narcissist, especially the superstar types, whether big time or small time. But we don't like to admit it.

Grace: I have a feeling that you're about to tell me to forget trying to break her spell—that there's too much going against it.

Bill: No, but you have more to do than handle Michelle. Narcissism or self-love is fashionable; TV is full of it. Michelle is part of a bigger problem. There is a way to handle her. It's simple really and begins with your being absolutely honest with yourself.

All her life, people have been throwing coals on her fire and wondering why it never goes out. You have to learn to rid yourself of those subtle feelings of identification. There's a part of you and your staff that is attracted to Michelle's self-love. If you can do it, the rest of your group will be empowered to do the same. It's those emotions—yours and the department's—that feed her narcissism.

Grace: I don't feel I should learn to dislike her or purposely become angry with her. Do you mean that?

Bill: No, all you need to learn is why you're drawn to her and then modify your own percpetion. The rest will follow automatically. Let's start with a questionnaire that will explore what about a narcissist is appealing. [See the boxed true/false questionnaire.]

THE WHITMAN (NOT CHOCOLATE)

Complete the following true/false questionnaire.

1. Achieving visible success is very important to me.   True   False
2. People see me as a natural leader.   True   False
3. I can't stand being alone.   True   False
4. I was my parent's favorite child.   True   False
5. I'd rather go to a social event than stay home and watch a good movie.   True   False
6. I make more calls to friends than most other people do.   True   False
7. I enjoy being around bright, attractive people.   True   False
8. I like being taken care of.   True   False
9. I can't stand the thought of being hurt in an accident.   True   False
10. I seldom go anywhere alone.   True   False

Examining the Clues: What Grace's Answers Mean

Grace circled "True" for every statement.

Grace: You don't have to say it. It's clear that I'm an easy mark for Michelle. Does it mean that I'm like her?

Bill: If it does, then so am I. My scores are like yours. Many people in service, public-oriented jobs share these same tendencies. We love to interact and influence others, and we don't mind being the center of attraction. That doesn't make us narcissists in the way Michelle is, but it does leave us vulnerable. Therefore, we have to guard against being conned. You know the expression: The easiest person to sell is a salesperson.

Grace: I follow you. I'll accept being vulnerable. What next? What do I do?

Bill: You don't want to reject or become angry with her or force her to quit or fire her. There's no justification for any of those alternatives right now. You've seen that you and the department are unknowing participants in feeding her narcissism. That is, she's getting all that attention, including attention from the top, for her "love-me" qualities. Notice what keeps the fire going: She needs, you give. Now, what do you think has to be done?

Cracking the Case: How Grace Can Break Michelle's Spell

Grace: It can't be stop giving and start rejecting; we've ruled that out in this workplace. What about giving something else? A substitute? What about that? Giving something else so that she doesn't have to respond as the narcissist? That's a mouthful. Giving what? Is there something in what I've said?

Bill: Absolutely. You've got it! Give her reasons to be appreciated that are more substantial and important to the department. To start you off, why don't you list what you believe to be Michelle's strong points, in addition to "love me."

Grace: 1. She has a lot of energy.
2. People flock to her.
3. She learns quickly.
4. She's a good presenter to a group.
5. She can do anything she sets her mind on.

Bill: Now try to devise something positive that Michelle can accomplish by leveraging each of those qualities.

Grace: 1. If Michelle could use her energy positively, she would be a top producer in the department.
2. If Michelle could rally people for constructive behaviors, she could become a leader in training.
3. If Michelle could learn some of the new processes quickly, she would help us increase quality.
4. If Michelle could present our results at executive conferences, she will make us look good as well as herself.
5. If Michelle could do all of the above, she would no longer constitute a problem.

Bill: What you have to do is create real assignments that correspond to any or all of the five points. Forget about the "love-me" person. Don't talk about or confront her with it or anything like that. No phrases like, "Do you remember what you used to be like?" Let that be history. Just let the natural events work their way into your and your department's perception of her. And those perceptions will change, believe us.

In battle they can be fearless, feeling they are invincible. In sports they can take chances and create new moves because they are confident of success. In work situations their underlying talents, once identified, can be used to advantage. They will be getting the same amount of attention and adulation but for substantive rather than selfish reasons.

There is a connection between a narcissist and a con. Cons and narcissists are both seductive people, and both want to

BREAKING THE NARCISSIST'S SPELL

List your narcissist's strong points:

1. _____
2. _____
3. _____
4. _____
5. _____

Identify something positive that the self-centered person in your workplace could accomplish by leveraging each of his or her positive qualities:

1. _____
2. _____
3. _____
4. _____
5. _____

Many narcissists have a great deal to give once their self-love doesn't cloud the observer's eyes to what is really there. Narcissists, because of their fixation on themselves, will go where more cautious and careful people fear to tread.

manipulate your behavior. Although true cons may share some qualities with the narcissist, they can't afford to engage in too much self-love. Too much self-love can blind them to their real purpose: to score, to call the mark out. In other words, the true con will know when to stop; the narcissist will not.

Michelle isn't the only kind of narcissist you may have to deal with. There are other varieties, both men and women, among all levels of management.

SOLUTIONS
What to Think

Michelle's case teaches a key lesson: The narcissist will get by your defenses no matter how vigilant you may be. Some narcissists are clever, seductive, and charming. Think:

"I'm enjoying this too much. Why? I have to take another look."

Some narcissists are so obviously in love with everything they do that you are repelled and angry, but they too can have something of value to offer once you look more deeply. The more you are turned off, the more demanding they will be. Their need for adulation will continue to escalate so that soon you will be wasting time and energy wondering about how to handle them. Think:

"They're getting too much of my attention. They've won. I've lost. I have to break the cycle."

What to Do

Refer to Michelle's case. Whatever the variety of narcissist you have to deal with, the first step is identifying your own reactions. Ask yourself, "What do I feel about this person?" Fill out the true/false questionnaire on page 51. The next step is to switch the narcissist into more productive behavior, *based on his or her strong points.* If the narcissist works for you, that should not be too difficult.

What if the narcissist is a coworker? You should be able identify his or her unutilized talents. Handling a project together where a positive (non-narcissistic) talent has a chance to be noticed by others is emphasized is one method.

The narcissist as a member of a team is another possibility. Build on what's already been discussed. The best model is Michelle's case. The team leader would do exactly what Grace did, but not in anger or retaliation. You are not battling the narcissist. You are leading the Michelles of the world into experiences where the open or subtle flaunting of self-love becomes less necessary for their self-esteem and identity.

Here are some phrases to use:

"You are so good at presenting material at our department conferences. Would you mind teaching that skill to some of the others?"

"Here are some rough ideas for next week's new team meeting. Could you expand on it, put it together, and present it? And by the way, would you be interested in helping me co-facilitate the group? I'll help you. Here's a manual to read in advance. Any questions, I'll be here."

"I'm preparing some role-plays to help our new team develop smooth relationships with one another. Would you mind playing a brief role of a timid person?"

CHAPTER 7

EXTREME COMPETITIVENESS

The world tolerates conceit from those who are successful, but not from anybody else.

—John Blake

The over-achieving supercompetitor may be exciting to read about, but would you want that person working next to you or living with you? Can there be too much of a good thing? Yes, there can.

We love winners. The adrenalin surge created by identifying with superachievers, whether from business or athletics, cannot be denied. The probability of the average person's ever becoming one of these heroes is exceedingly small, yet the fact that heroes exist spurs us on. They become models, mentors, and coaches. Some people, though, become driven toward success, to the detriment of themselves and those they love.

Heroes seen at a distance always appear to have no flaws. Unfortunately, a few nationally acclaimed winners prove to have profound flaws. Local winners, who may be friends or neighbors, can also share the weaknesses of their larger-than-life nationally admired counterparts.

But what's the problem? If someone is very competitive, why not let him or her be? Why should it matter?

This is why: Extremely competitive people can stretch themselves to the breaking point, negatively affect the stability of their family, and disrupt the efficiency of others at work. Research shows that it is dangerous to your health to be too competitive. But health questions aside, how do you handle someone whose competitiveness negatively affects your own work?

THE CASE OF CINDY AND THE FEARSOME FOE

Cindy enters. "I'm not going to put up with him anymore, I swear I'm not. I don't care what he does or says, it's enough! He's too pushy and conceited." Cindy is a charged-up, obviously excited woman in her early thirties. A tailored, dark conservative suit creates the frame for gray-green eyes and pale skin. She has been waiting for what seemed to her to be a long time and doesn't like it.

"You'll have to forgive me for being impatient," she says, moving toward a chair, sighing, and smiling. "May I? But it's been some week."

She has a lot of energy and proves to be a quick-witted, humorous person.

Cindy: I came here because I'm afraid I'm getting to be too much like Keith, my partner at work. We're both competitive, but he overdoes it. We're on a fast track. I know he alienates more people than I do. I'm a nice competitor; he's an angry and abusive one.

Bill: And what do you do?

Cindy: I'm an attorney. You know what pressure that is.

Bill: Sure, but every industry and profession is under pressure. In today's economy the competition to succeed is ferocious. Can you give me an example of a typical incident that upsets you?

Cindy: Well, here's a current one. It has to do with my impossible colleague, Keith. There are five of us working on different parts of a large report, and the sections do not overlap. Once our work is finished, a committee will integrate the whole thing, and our names will be mentioned only as contributors.

Bill: But that committee will be able to judge the quality of what everyone turns in, so competition is built into the assignment.

Cindy: Correct. Keith does more than compete. He goes out of his way to downgrade the rest of us to our faces, saying things like, "You'll never finish on time. Sure you don't want some help?" And every chance he gets, he's brown-nosing the partners. If I ask him for some information, you would think I asked him for his right arm. But when he asks *me* for something, he snarls until he gets it. When he talks about our competition at department meetings, he's the first one to yell, "We'll kill 'em!" He's a pusher—not for the firm but for himself. I've watched him operate, and it turns my stomach.

Bill: You are both competitive. Something about his kind really gets to you. You probably know there are healthy and unhealthy kinds of competitive feelings. You are assuming that yours are healthy and his are not. Let's see if that's true. Here's a competitiveness questionnaire [see the box]. Rate each of the statements on a scale of 1 to 3: 1 for not true, 2 for somewhat true, and 3 for always true. Complete it first for yourself, and second for how Keith might answer.

COMPETITIVENESS QUESTIONNAIRE

Rate each statement on a scale of 1 to 3: 1 for not true, 2 for somewhat true, and 3 for always true.

	You	Someone Else
1. I need a challenge to keep me feeling alive.		
2. Others see me as very aggressive.		
3. When I feel strongly, I get it off my chest right away.		
4. I intimidate people.		
5. I am very impatient.		
6. No matter what, winning is everything.		

7. Controlling my temper is difficult.

8. I enjoy confrontations.

9. People see me as destined for big things.

10. I'm loaded with energy.

Cindy filled out the questionnaire quickly. Here are her answers:

	Cindy	Keith
1. I need a challenge to keep me feeling alive.	2	3
2. Others see me as very aggressive.	3	3
3. When I feel strongly, I get it off my chest right away.	2	3
4. I intimidate people.	2	3
5. I am very impatient.	2	3
6. No matter what, winning is everything.	1	3
7. Controlling my temper is difficult	2	3
8. I enjoy confrontations.	2	3
9. People see me as destined for big things.	2	3
10. I'm loaded with energy.	2	2

Examining the Clues: What Cindy's Answers Mean

Bill: You rate Keith as much more competitive than yourself. We don't know how he might rate himself or you, but the important finding is that you perceive a large difference. Yet even so, I have to ask why it bothers you so much.

Cindy: I don't begrudge him his possible success, but not at the expense of my own career or my own mental health.

Kathy: What do you mean by mental health? I can see your concern about your career, but being part of a high-pressure field was your own decision. Perhaps Keith is just the worst example of what can exist in the legal profession. Maybe you just got unlucky.

Cindy: If that were the case, I'd know it. After all, I've been around lawyers for eight years now. No, there's something wrong, and it may be me. I've got to learn how to handle Keith and all the others like him. The mental health thing? I'm afraid I might let down and not be as sharp as I should.

Bill: All right Cindy, let's see how you really feel about extremely competitive people. Here's a list of open-ended sentences [see the box]. Just complete them with the first thing that comes to mind.

"WANNA FIGHT?" QUESTIONNAIRE

Complete the following items.

1. Competitive people are _____

2. The difference between fair and unfair competition is _____

3. The "mean" competitor is _____

4. If I were married to a "mean" competitor _____

Cindy made these responses:

---

1. Competitive people are *exciting and motivating to be around.*

2. The difference between fair and unfair competition is *that the unfair competitor can hurt you.*

3. The "mean" competitor is *dangerous.*

Some medical and psychological researchers feel that there is a pathological competition whose consequences include an increased probability of heart attacks—so-called Type A personalities. It's a field of inquiry that goes back thirty years and is always being refined and focused. The current thinking is that the Type A component that does the damage is "po-

4. If I were married to a "mean" competitor *I'd have to let him dominate me to please him, or I'd have to leave.*
5. If a "mean" competitor really lost control *he could kill someone.*

Bill: Do I have to spell it out? You are literally in fear for your life. You see Keith as potentially dangerous. It's no wonder you are having trouble. He has walled you off with the hostility you pick up as part of what drives his competitiveness. You're left with no way to interact with him, or even make the first attempt to handle the problem. Your first goal has to be getting yourself ready to be proactive and not run away.

Cindy: You're right, but the guy's an ogre. And you want me to get close and interact with him?

Bill: Would you prefer to quit?

Cindy: You know I won't do that.

Bill: I'm with you. You are now going to practice what you should do. Here's the scene. You are ready to go to work. You stop at the front door, look into the hall mirror, and make a face that reminds you of Keith at his worst. Can you do that now?

Cindy: OK, here, I've made the face. Horrible isn't it? Now what do I do?

Bill: Now close your eyes and tell Keith exactly what you think of him—all the stuff you've been saving up, no matter what it is. Blurt it out. You can. And enjoy it.

What do you think about the overly competitive person in your workplace?

_____

_____

_____

Cindy: Just let me at him! Here goes:

tential for hostility." If you are placed in a position where you must work with a highly competitive person, look for the hostility factor. Defusing the hostility could add years to that person's life. We don't expect you to be the diagnostician. All you need to do, whether you smell hostility or not, is reduce the pressure— for the other person and on yourself.

Just one more time you push me aside or ignore me, humiliate me, and make me feel like I don't belong—you mean little rat—you're getting the same treatment. It's *you* who doesn't belong. You don't fit! You mediocre, bullying, S-O-B.

Cracking the Case: How Cindy Can Get Keith to Back Off

Bill: You're all charged up. Let's get back to reality. Now pretend you are at work and that you and Keith are seated across a desk holding the report material you were talking about. Keith says something like, "Hey, Cindy, I know you're not too busy. How about taking a look at this material? There's one part there—you'll find it—that needs your soft touch. Polish it up, will ya? I did all the real work anyway. Call me when it's finished—but not too long."

How would you respond to Keith in this situation? Say what you're really thinking. This is just a rehearsal.

How would you respond to Keith in this situation?

_____

_____

_____

Cindy fired off this response:

It's time you did your own word housekeeping. I'm too stupid, remember? Look for favors from someone you treat better than me. By the way, I don't think you'll find anyone who fits that category around here. You've made so many friends. I know. Why don't you try the president's secretary?

SOLUTIONS

What to Think

The solution starts, as dramatized, with recognizing and confronting your own fears. Suppose there is a Keith-type person in your office. He will keep people away because he's too hot to handle, which gives him a clear field for his own ambitions. Breaching that wall of angry energy is the first step. Think this:

> "If I let someone like you push me around and frighten me away with your crazy antics, loud noises, and angry faces, what respect can I have for myself?"

The natural tendency is to give overly-competitive people a taste of their own medicine, matching their emotional pushing and shoving with your own. That will seldom work. What you

Today's high-stress work environment is a perfect arena for the success-driven, overly competitive person. If you are running scared, for whatever reason, you will be fair game. This person wants you to believe you will lose and will act as if you've already lost. That's the bully element. Think this:

> "I may be uptight, but I'm not stupid. If you think I'm going to stand still and be eaten alive, you've picked the wrong person."

What to Do

Cindy did it by refusing to be demeaned and sarcastically confronted Keith with his negative reputation. If the overly competitive person happens to be your boss, however, you need a different game plan. You must protect your job (assuming you don't want to quit) *and* your self-esteem.

must do is get to the heart of the effect they have on you— inducing fear and anxiety and making you angry— and show that you are not afraid, cannot be intimi- dated, and will not be provoked.

In terms of job security, show your boss that you are indispensable. That's important because if your boss is ambitious, he or she will need your ability to further his or her own goals. Once that's done, your self-esteem will be strengthened by accepting that you won't be emotionally pushed around and that you don't intend to be eaten alive.

You are probably thinking that this is all easier said than done, and it is, just as it is for so many other prescriptions for a healthier life. Yet there is a way, and it goes beyond thinking—which is only the first, but necessary step.

You have to see why you react to the boss, coworker, or other person of this type as you do. What do we mean by "see"? Look at, "see," the answers to the sentence items you responded to on pages 59–60. Take a small mental step. "See" those responses as objectively as possible—which is to say, as you are looking at yourself. Be the self-analyzer. Do that, and you will get a clue about why the extremely competitive person gets under your skin.

Now for actual tactics:

- Never get angry.
- Look, act, and dress as if you have just received a prize assignment or have just been promoted to the job you've always wanted. In other words, don't communicate a losing and frightened image.
- Stop at the mirror in the hall and conjure up the face of the person who's making your life miserable. Then get it off your chest—explode, be cynical, tease, provoke, or whatever else you find easiest to do.

At home rearrange your apartment, buy some new prints or paintings for the walls, new CDs, switch to more assertive clothes and colors. At work, come in looking as if you control the place. Get your work done—more than the required amount—and leave as if you still control the place.

It's a mind game, but you have to do it because your job and self-esteem may be on the line. In time you will begin to regard yourself differently—as more confident, with more power, and a greater capacity to handle that S-O-B.

CHAPTER 8

OVERCONTROLLING

We brought in a group of university consultants to help our executives figure out what our values are. Then we tested the employees, and if they didn't buy into those values, we knew they wouldn't work out.

—CEO of a Fortune 500 company

If you discover that your decisions are having less and less significance and you're told it's the way things are being restructured, you're being controlled—too controlled.

The overcontrolling person, whether CEO or coworker, pushes you further and further into a corner. You look for a way around a force of personality that becomes almost physical. Words like *suffocating* and *stifling* have been used to describe the overcontrolling person's effect on others.

Is overcontrol the same as restructuring? It could be. Sometimes it's difficult to differentiate the two. Here's how. Some leaders who can't trust their employees at all will be heard to say things like, "Well, we can't operate without a plan, can we?"

Control this, control that—hierarchies, bureaucracies. Why the compulsion to control? Because when the lid's off, so some think, there's no telling what people might do, and the more one has to lose, the more control seems to be needed over others.

Control—overcontrol—is a power to be reckoned with, for who can tell what dangerous emotions and feelings might otherwise be unleashed? In the workplace, it ruins relationships and stifles creativity.

THE CASE OF TRACEY AND WILMA WITCH

Tracey shows up at the end of the day. "I'm beat," she says, "not from waiting in line here but from the terrible thoughts about my teammate going around and around in my head." Tracey is a small woman in her early thirties. She stands sure-footed and defiant. "Do you mind if I stand and walk around a little?" and so she does. "I've got to get her out of my system. I feel trapped just thinking about her." She smiles, stretches slowly like someone who has just awakened, and sits down. "OK. I'm ready."

She tells us about someone called Wilma Witch, a fictitious name, "but a real person—too real to me." Tracy and Wilma had been assigned to work together to solve a recurring quality problem. They were selected because of their superior performance in different parts of their plant and because they did not know one another. Both women had the reputation of being tough, unyielding, and painfully truthful about quality standards. The trouble between them began almost immediately.

Kathy: It's obvious that working with Wilma isn't the highlight of your day—that you're upset and don't like it. Tell us how you see the problem.

Tracey: "See" is not strong enough. I *feel* the problem: in my head, my heart, my bones. I'm ready to burst. You're a counselor. Can someone who makes you feel about a foot high actually affect your love life?

Kathy: If you mean can someone who demeans you and drains your energy affect your physical well-being, the answer is yes. But what exactly do you feel? What's going on?

Tracey: Well, here it is, blow by blow. I used to feel on top of things. I knew what I was doing, did it well, and enjoyed myself. I liked the people around me, and I knew they liked me. It was a pleasure helping them. Now I'm getting headaches, stomachaches, and worse.

With Wilma Witch—it makes me feel good to

say her name that way—I've turned into one of those
dominated children you read about: can't think for myself, triple-check everything, wonder whether she's
going to approve or yell at me. But I never was a dominated child, and I'm not going to become one to please
her. I hate it!

She has a great reputation. She's supposed to be
next in line for the quality assurance manager's job.
Boy, is that going to ruin things around there, if that
ever happens.

Kathy: You can't stand her. You don't like what she's doing
to you. You're not functioning like you used to. It's
time to do something about it.

Tracey: I like the sound of that. She's an overcontrolling
monster as far as I'm concerned. I don't figure she's
going to change. I certainly don't plan to leave, and I'm
not going to change to accommodate her. There's a big
job they've given the two of us. How do we do it?

This is a rock-and-a-hard-place scenario. The work environment is intolerable because of an unyielding, difficult
person, while the aggravated employee is equally unyielding. What makes this situation particularly stressful is that
overcontrolling behavior can be both mind and body
smashing.

Tracey is a strong person, and even she discovers negative
consequences in many areas of her life. Think of those who
aren't strong to begin with or who themselves may have
been raised in an overcontrolling home environment. For
such people, the kind of interaction between Tracey and
Wilma can be disastrous. Helping such people free themselves from the domination of an overcontrolling coworker
or boss can be lifesaving. What we are going to suggest and
outline for Tracey applies equally to everyone who finds
their identities similarly diminished.

Kathy: We don't want you to think there's anything seriously wrong with you because of the way you've re-
acted to Wilma. Don't blame yourself. What's

happened is that you're caught in a relationship you can't get out of. You feel dominated and terribly vulnerable. You and Wilma represent the model for millions who are trapped in dead-end relationships. *Remember this idea: You're trapped and can't see a way out.* If you could find a way out, there would be much less of a problem. Wilma would merely be another blip on your screen of life.

Tracey: Got it. I have to make Wilma into a blip on my TV screen of life, not to see her as a deep problem but as a minor irritation. How?

Kathy: Bravo! We're together on that one. Now on to the solution. Think of a situation where Wilma could be the blip.

Tracey: Where she's not in charge.

Kathy: Good. Another?

Tracey: Where she's in a crowd.

Kathy: Great. You've found the goals: less power over others and being one of many. Now for the fun part— making it happen.

Tracey: That's where you come in. What's the magic?

Kathy: I'll follow your own insights. First, diminishing the impact of her power: I want to explore your ideas about overcontrolling people with power.

Tracey: Ready.

"DO YOU HAVE AN IMAGE OF SOMEONE'S HEAD IN A VISE" QUESTIONNAIRE

Complete the following sentences with your first thought.

1. When someone dictates and controls my behavior I feel _____

2. Being controlled by others is _____

3. A controlling person is _____

4. A controlling person reminds me of _____

5. The reason I feel trapped by a controlling person is _____

6. Controlling people behave that way because ___
_____

7. I need someone to control me because _____
_____

8. Overcontrolling people should not be in positions of leadership because _____

9. Overcontrolling people are _____

10. If I could say whatever I wished to an overcontrolling person, I would say _____

We gave Tracey the sentence-completion shown in the box. Here are her responses:

1. When someone dictates and controls my behavior I feel *small and insignificant, like why am I here?*
2. Being controlled by others *is an awful experience.*
3. A controlling person is *hard to fight.*
4. A controlling person reminds me of *a devil, a witch, a dragon, someone who isn't even human.*
5. The reason I feel trapped by a controlling person is *that they have the power to hurt me if I try to escape their influence.*
6. Controlling people behave that way because *they don't trust anyone and have to second-guess everything and need to dominate.*
7. I need someone to control me because *Wrong, I don't need anyone to control me.*
8. Overcontrolling people should not be in positions of leadership because *they ruin my motivation.*
9. Overcontrolling people are *not healthy to be around.*
10. If I could say whatever I wished to an overcontrolling person, I would say, "*If you can't stop dominating me and learn to trust my decisions I'm out of here. You are going to end up being alone and miserable and you'll bring it on yourself.*"

Examining the Clues: What Tracey's Answers Mean

Kathy: What you've revealed is that you are afraid of being injured by something that's almost supernatural. You have to get away. You're diminished, and you can't stand being in her presence. It's no wonder you're having difficulty. In your eyes, Wilma is dragon lady.

Tracey: I did say those things. But I still can't understand my reaction to her. She really can't hurt me—or can she?

Kathy: The clue is that you don't want to fail on the job you share with her. You have to work together. If you didn't care, you'd walk, but you're not going to do that. You're too good and want to stick it out. Yet working with Wilma prevents you from exercising the freedom you want. No freedom, no self-esteem, no Tracey as you know yourself—therefore the headaches and those other disturbing physical symptoms.

Tracey: You're telling me I'm trapped in an irrational, childish fear, that Wilma isn't really a dragon lady.

Kathy: You said it. She truly isn't what you think she is. So now we know that Wilma's a plain, ordinary overcontrolling human being with whom you have the misfortune of being temporarily paired. The next step is losing her in a crowd.

Cracking the Case: How Tracey Can Turn Around Wilma's Wicked Ways

Tracey: How are you going to make that work?

Kathy: That's really easy. Take this form [see the box] and fill it in. There are eleven lines. In the left-hand column, list the names of ten people you like and who are important to you. Put Wilma's name on line 11. Next to each name, write down why those people are important. We've already handled Wilma, so fill in that line too.

"RELATIONSHIPS AND MEANINGS" QUESTIONNAIRE

Prepare a list of ten people who are important to you, and put your overcontrolling person on line 11.

	Name	Why This Person Is Important
1.	_____	_____
2.	_____	_____
3.	_____	_____
4.	_____	_____
5.	_____	_____
6.	_____	_____
7.	_____	_____
8.	_____	_____
9.	_____	_____
10.	_____	_____
11.	_____	_____
	[Name of the overcontrolling person]	

Tracey's list looked like this:

	Name	Why This Person Is Important
1.	*My mother*	*She loves me. I love her.*
2.	*My father*	*Trustworthy, someone I can confide in.*
3.	*Roger*	*Couldn't ask for a nicer boyfriend.*
4.	*Francine*	*Happy, spontaneous, makes me feel good.*
5.	*Catherine*	*We share things together, confidante.*

6.	*Glenn*	*A rock; we grew up together.*
7.	*Jack*	*My mentor at school.*
8.	*Sally*	*My assistant, a jewel to work with.*
9.	*Sergio*	*My boss; taught me to trust others.*
10.	*Michael*	*My lovable favorite uncle.*
11.	*Wilma*	*The dragon lady who scares me.*

Kathy: That list you've completed is a sample of your universe of relationships. Take a good look at it. Now look at Wilma's line. Do you mean to tell me that Wilma can influence your behavior more than all the others combined? She's coming up too big on your screen of life. Put her back where she belongs. She's a blip, and that's all.

Tracey: Wilma? Who's Wilma? What Wilma?

SOLUTIONS

What to Think

The over-controlling person drains your energies and forces you to fight a rearguard action to avoid being overwhelmed.

Therefore, the first step, as demonstrated through Tracey's case history, is to free yourself mentally from being suffocated. Think this:

"I'll never become the person I can be so long as I let him or her dominate and control me."

Think about what's been happening to you. The chances are good that you:

- Don't laugh and smile as much as you used to.
- Are afraid of things that you once were able to handle with ease.

- Are irritating your friends.
- Assume that you've made a mistake when you haven't.
- Look and act older than you are.

Need we go on? Think this:

> "The overcontrolling person is a demon disguised as a normal human being. I don't need demons in my life. Out, out!"

Is *demon* too harsh? Here's the dictionary definition: "an evil spirit; a source or agent of evil, harm, distress, or ruin." The overcontrolling person is evil because your capacity to live your life and grow has been harmed. You are in distress. Your future could well be ruined.

What to Do

We brought Tracey up to the point at which our counseling ended. We did *not* tell her what to do. She gained strength from the recognition of what was happening to her and why it spelled disaster. This is what she did.

The very next day, she walked into Wilma's office and announced that since they had equal status and responsibilities, she (Tracey) was going to record their independent and joint decisions. She suggested that Wilma do the same. At the end of each day, they could compare their data and discuss and resolve any differences.

What could Wilma do but agree? After all, Tracey's proposal was taken straight from concepts of measurement and quality assurance, and they were both supposed to be experts in that field. The ploy lasted only a week. After that time, and together with her more realistic mental attitude, Wilma was no longer difficult to deal with.

We've shown you what can be done when a coworker is involved. Suppose the overcontrolling person is your boss. That's an entirely different ballgame. Straightening out your attitude is always the first step. Once that's accomplished, you'll be better able to think more clearly about your options.

The options in dealing with an overcontrolling boss are close to those recommended for an overly competitive boss. Those two types are far from the same kinds of people, yet—and this is very important—their effects on you can be very similar.

The chances that an overcontrolling boss is going to change are very slim. Why should he or she? This person has power and the gratification that comes with self-expressing themselves freely. Protecting your sense of self is critical. Reread the suggestions at the end of the chapter about extreme competitiveness—and do it in spades. Your goal is to reduce the pressure, to get out from under being dominated. Completely? That's not very likely. Significantly? Yes, enough to reclaim your energy in order to make realistic plans and search for alternatives.

You've worked on your self-esteem and are mentally prepared to handle your overcontrolling difficult person. Here are some suggestions about what to do next:

- *A coworker:* Work at your own pace; smile; give feedback; behave as if he or she is the most normal, nicest person in the world. Say, "I appreciate all your help and advice. Let me do it my way. You wouldn't want me to be all over your back. Relax. We'll get more done."
- *A boss:* The game plan is for you to get out from under. The best ploy is for you to become a moving target—hard to follow and track down. This is how: Provide a lot of feedback; document; make many suggestions; be pleasant and cooperative—and firm—about what you can and cannot do. Suggest this and that; be here and there; be busy; modify a request ("Have you thought of this . . . ?") or add your own twist ("What if we do it this way?").

CHAPTER 9

IT TAKES TWO TO MAKE A TOADY

But when I tell him he hates flatterers.
He says he does, being then most flattered.

—Shakespeare, *Julius Caesar*

How do you spot a toadie? There are three ways: kinesthetic, linguistic, and olfactory—how they move, talk, and smell. We're sure you've observed all three. The yes-man takes on the walk and gestures of the boss, begins to use similar words and phrasing, and even wears the same scent.

Like a particle drawn to a magnet, the yes-man, toady, sycophant, draws energy from the leader. Turn the magnetic field off, and the toady falls to the ground like a lifeless puppet, looking foolish and disjointed.

Insecure leaders need them; great leaders despise them.

Toadies aspire to leadership. Upon achieving power, they spawn more toadies, who in turn give birth to multitudes, until finally the whole organization moves, talks, and smells alike. Then what? It's bought out, goes bankrupt, and becomes an example of how *not* to conduct a business.

THE CASE OF JOE, THE MAN IN THE EMPTY SUIT

Joe, fashioned by Brooks Brothers, neat and conforming, moves into the room cautiously. Nothing is out of place. Joe's problem is himself. He can't get out of the habit of thinking first what the boss is about to think and later never being sure what his own ideas are, or if he has any. In a meeting he would look at the boss, know what *he* would say, and say it. Then the boss would say, "My thoughts exactly, Joe."

Joe: I'm sent to meetings because I will say his words. Everyone hates me. They can't afford to hate him. This is some life. He gets the glory, compensation, and benefits, and I get to lose my personality. Oh well, it's better than a stick in the eye.

Kathy: Everyone who has come in here has complained about someone else. You're saying *you* are the difficult person. It's unusual and you are welcome. How do you think others see you?

Joe: You know the expression, "with fear and loathing." Plus they think I'm selfish. Imagine that, selfish. I really care only about *him*. I'm his right-hand man, his Boswell. His wish is my desire. Of course, he's promised I'll be his heir, and that's worth waiting for. But, for insurance, I'd like to learn how to get my personality back—if I can still find it. As for the other folks, I don't care if they don't like or respect me. They've got their own problems.

Kathy: Before we talk about getting a personality back, why don't we find out what you're getting out of your present role as the boss's yes-man. Is that the right word?

Joe: I've been called worse: toady, sycophant, and you know what. I know I flatter him, but honestly, I do like and respect the guy. He can be inspiring.

Kathy: Do you mind filling in these sentence-completion items about your boss and yourself? [see the box]. Just write the first thing that comes to mind.

These are Joe's responses:

---

1. My boss (list five):
   Is like a mother and father to me.
   Has my career in his hands.
   Can become one of this country's great leaders.
   Needs me.
   Knows I will do anything to protect him.
2. If my boss were to get hurt *I think I'd feel the same amount of pain.*
3. What I dread most is *falling out of favor with my boss.*

THE "K.A." QUESTIONNAIRE

You may be too infatuated with a leader. Fill in the form below to discover if you are in danger of being submerged by your leader's personality. For this questionnaire, you should pretend that your boss is the most important person in the world.

1. My boss (list five qualities):

    _____

    _____

    _____

    _____

    _____

2. If my boss were to get hurt _____

3. What I dread most is _____

4. My boss trusts me because _____

5. My boss expects me to _____

6. When I look in the mirror, I see (list five things):

    _____

    _____

    _____

    _____

    _____

7. I need my boss because _____

8. I love my boss because _____

9. If my boss determined he had to fire me to save his career _____

    _____

10. If my boss told me I would not inherit his job ___

    _____

4. My boss trusts me because *I will do anything he asks without question and keep my mouth shut.*
5. My boss expects me to *inherit his job.*
6. When I look in the mirror I see (list five):
   My boss.
   A successful man.
   Sometimes nothing.
   A phony.
   A child's face.
7. I need my boss because *without him I'd be nothing.*
8. I love my boss because *he loves me.*
9. If my boss determined he had to fire me to save his career *I would probably agree.*
10. If my boss told me I would not inherit his job *I can't finish that sentence.*

Dr. Faustus makes a pact with the devil and trades his soul to have his every wish fulfilled. Joe is doing the same thing. In this modern version, the toady, yes-man, trades his or her identity (personality, as Joe refers to it) for the promise of power.

Examining the Clues: What Joe's Responses Mean

Kathy: What it all boils down to, Joe, is that your boss exists; therefore you exist. So of course you feel you don't have a personality. But let me ask you something. Suppose that tomorrow you learn that he has disappeared, and the board, of which you're a member, names you his successor. Would you take the job knowing what you now know about yourself?

Joe: In a minute. I've always said I wanted that job. I'll worry about the personality part later. I want the power.

Kathy: But is power a personality?

Joe: It's said that people in power grow into their jobs. I can do that.

Kathy: In other words, if you knew all that power would be coming, you wouldn't be here.

Joe: I'm afraid that's true. It would be, "So long Kathy, I'm out of here. See you when I'm in real trouble."

We've developed the situation to the point of the classic Faustian scenario.

But suppose power isn't attainable—because of a restructuring program, perhaps, or a merger or buyout. The sycophant is left high and dry. What becomes of the trade-off? There are two possibilities: the well-trained yes-man can attach himself or herself to another sponsor, or he or she may be forced to find that lost personality. It's the latter—how to begin the search for the lost personality—that I will help Joe confront next.

Kathy: Try this possibility. Your company's sold, there are new leaders, you're out—and your old boss is floating happily in his golden parachute and waves as you look up. Then what?

Joe: I'd come in here screaming, "Kathy, help me."

Kathy: Then we'd have to begin finding out who you really are. Do you think you want to stand on your own feet?

Joe: I wish I could answer that. All I know is that without a sponsor, I'd be in deep trouble. It could take up to a year for someone like me to find the right job. I'd better do something for myself for a change.

Kathy: So we're agreed. The search for Joe begins. Think about who you'd like to be—your ideal self, the person you have always wished to be.

Joe: If I try to imagine my ideal person, I see only my boss. Ugh, that's not me. I don't really want to be him.

Kathy: Look, there's nothing wrong with using your boss as a model. What you need to do is consider being like your boss on your own terms, not through the route of a yes-man. If anyone should know his strong and weak points, it's you. You can work on both. You might even outdo him.

Joe: I sensed you were clever. You're proposing that not only do I give up being his toadie but that I also work on surpassing him. I tell you, it's a great feeling thinking about it. What a relief. Why not? Why shouldn't I try doing it?

Kathy: Now try this next exercise, listing your boss's weak and strong points [see the box].

SO LONG, K.A.

List five strong points and five weak points for the person you admire.

Weak Points

1. _____
2. _____
3. _____
4. _____
5. _____

Strong Points

1. _____
2. _____
3. _____
4. _____
5. _____

Joe listed the following points for his boss:

Weak Points
1. *He needs people around him, like me, who scrape and bow.*
2. *He gets depressed when he's not the center of attention.*
3. *He has a lousy family life.*
4. *He can really slice someone up.*
5. *He really doesn't trust anyone.*

Strong Points
1. *He's very bright.*
2. *He's incredibly well organized.*
3. *He has a fantastic memory for just about everything.*
4. *He can charm audiences and employees.*
5. *He'll do anything when he thinks it's good for the company.*

Cracking the Case: How Joe Can Learn to Be His Own Man

Kathy: Look at your lists, Joe. Is there any reason that you have to buy the whole package? Your boss's positive qualities are admirable, and we can see why people are drawn to him. But the negatives! Imagine yourself with the positives but without the negatives.

Joe: How long will such a change take?

Kathy: It will be a never-ending challenge. That's what makes life interesting. The choice is still in your hands. All I've done is help you look at what's going on and what the alternatives may be. I'm not deserting you. If you need some help with your change process, get back in line whenever you wish. I'll be here.

Joe was left hanging, although with more insight. He called a week later, and this is what he reported: He realized that it took two to make a toady. His boss needed a yes-man. But did he, Joe, need to be a true toady? Could he disentangle himself slowly while still giving his boss the yes-man qualities he wanted? He decided he could, for a time, play the toady role without losing his personality in the process. There wasn't one event, statement, or dramatic switch in his behavior. The process was gradual. It was started and continued going on inside Joe's head.

There are degrees of toadyism, not as pure as Joe's case, that deserve our attention next. Many employees drift into a yes-man role without realizing it; others do so very consciously. These are the more common reasons:

- *Job protection:* Being safe under someone's wing.
- *Stress reduction:* Why make waves? Be agreeable.
- *Career advancement:* If he or she likes me, I may have an edge.
- *A cover:* While looking for another job.

SOLUTIONS

What to Think

We armed Joe with a clear set of options, which included the possibility of his outdoing his leader. Therefore, learning from the man in the empty suit, think this:

"Is it worth losing my personality to achieve success?"

Joe wasn't completely convinced. Becoming a toady like Joe—regard him as a professional—isn't a quality that appears suddenly. It's a carefully cultivated set of responses, of cleverly thought-out maneuvers and manipulations, because, as Joe reported, you are not everyone's favorite person. In spite of that, however, the toady can rise in the organization or, at worst, protect his position.

Toadies, as Joe discovered, have few friends. Once again a trade-off is involved. Think this:

"Am I willing to put up with other people's anger and ridicule—to be the person they joke about—trying to get what may or may not ever be there?"

If you discover you're becoming a yes-man and don't like it, explore your feelings and find out why. It may be one of the reasons in the list you just read. The toady tactic may be the correct one so long as you don't get to like it too much. Think this:

"I don't like yes-men. I don't want to become one, but if I have to pretend to be a toady to save myself, I will."

What to Do

Let's restate what's been happening in this chapter. The difficult person is you. Your spouse, or girlfriend or boyfriend, has given you an ultimatum: "I'm not living with a sycophant" (toady to you).

Self-discovery is always the first step in your process of rehabilitation. If you are a toady, or near-toady, admit it. Do the sentence completion exercise in the box as honestly as you can to gain insight into yourself.

MIRROR, MIRROR, ON THE WALL

1. I've drifted into being a yes-man because _____
   _____

2. If I became assertive and stood up for what I believed _____

3. I may really need the protection of a stronger person because _____

4. If I knew I'd get that promotion, being a yes-man
   _____

5. Your closest friend says, "I don't like people who toady up to others." Your response is: _____
   _____

What do you see in your responses? Are you pleased with yourself? Are you ashamed, or do you feel you're the realistic one? Whatever your answer—"I like," "I don't like," or "I'm doing it as a conscious tactic"—be honest.

CHAPTER 10

LESSONS: HANDLING ALL KINDS OF DIFFICULT PEOPLE

How can methods for dealing with examples of nine difficult people serve as the building blocks for literally hundreds of irritating behaviors? Not so strange. The early Greeks thought that four humors—hostility, apathy, depression, and enthusiasm (in today's terms)—could account for all behavior. The Ten Commandments constitute a small list as well. Freud suggested three driving forces: the id, ego, and superego. Jung added the concepts of two others: introvert and extrovert. Personality type theorists propose anywhere from four to eight building blocks.

One major category is missing from this book: the enthusiastic, happy, energetic person—in other words, the life-embracing, cheerful individual. Those are not "difficult" attitudes. But in today's society, a truly cheerful person might be regarded as being out of step. We don't think so.

HOW TO TURN NINE INTO HUNDREDS

Unlike as in novels, you meet few people in most self-help books; insights and advice are handed down to you. We've never felt comfortable with that approach. Practice the techniques you need to handle difficult people in your worklife, remembering Joe, Tracey, Cindy, Grace, Fred, Red, Ron, George, and Margaret. Of course, the relationships you have with difficult people will be unique, as is every relationship. The trick is to remember the techniques used in these chapters for overcoming the situations.

RELATIONSHIPS CAN ONLY BE CHANGED ONE AT A TIME

There are no one-size-fits-all answers. Each angry person or overcontrolling person needs to be dealt with individually. The problems and resolutions in this book work for the specific examples presented in the chapters. Yet although the answers may not always be the same, the methods for finding the answer are. The questionnaires in the chapters will help you explore why a difficult relationship exists and how to improve it, or at least protect yourself from it. As you learn how to handle each difficult person in your life, you'll be better armed to handle the next, and the next.

CHANGE STARTS FROM THE DISTRESSED PERSON'S SIDE

Since you think a problem exists, *you* are the distressed person. Change begins when you realize that something is wrong and you find yourself thinking about a miserable situation, talking about it to a friend or family member, or even visiting a counselor.

Your first thought is usually to get rid of the irritant. Then you realize that the difficult person can't easily be eliminated. Worse, the difficult person isn't about to change. Why should he or she?

Then comes the next thought, "What can I do? This is driving me crazy." It's at that point that each chapter began. The distressed person—you in this case—had to obtain a better understanding of the reasons for irritation than what he or she came in with.

The specific methods in each case may be different, depending on the kind of difficult person being handled, but the approach and attack on the problem were similar. Those steps, with explanations, are listed below.

1. Look more deeply into yourself and consider how you feel about and react to the difficult behavior. Identify the real problem and why the situation bothers you. The question of what it all means has to be answered first.
2. Experiments and exercises—completing sentences, creating mock conversations, charting graphs, and making ratings—prepare you to handle your particular difficult person.
3. Crack the case and figure out the actual solution for the difficult person in your life.

WHY IT CAN WORK FOR YOU

You will remember these stories—Margaret's mean and angry manager, Red's cynical manager, Ron's pessimists, and Joe's lost personality, to name a few. Put yourself into the roles of these nine people. With those models in mind, confront other difficult people using the same methods. The box lists other kinds of difficult behaviors. Next to each, we note the chapters from which hints for better handling can be derived.

ADDITIONAL CATEGORIES OF DIFFICULT PEOPLE

Unresponsive	See Chapters 5, 3, and 2.
Negative	See Chapters 2 and 3.
Know-It-All	See Chapters 1, 6, 7, and 8.
Indecisive	See Chapters 2, 3, and 4.
Complainer	See Chapters 1, 2, 4, and 7.
Sneak	See Chapters 1, 2, 7, and 8.
Whiner	See Chapters 2, 3, and 4.
Politician	See Chapters 1, 4, 6, 7, and 8.

Manipulator	See Chapters 1, 4, 6, 7, 8, and 9.
Procrastinator	See Chapters 2, 3, and 4.
Staller	See Chapters 2, 4, and 9.
Exploder	See Chapters 1, 7, and 8.
Sniper	See Chapters 1, 2, 7, 8, and 9.
Sarcastic	See Chapters 1, 4, 6, 7, and 8.
Thin-Skinned	See Chapters 2, 5, and 9.